WHEN THERAPY
DOESN'T WORK

T0273345

WHEN THERAPY DOESN'T WORK

A Mindfulness Guide to Emotional Repair

SHELLY YOUNG LPC LISAC,
SHINZEN YOUNG
WITH ELIZABETH RENINGER

TRIGGER
The mental health & well-being publisher

Published in 2024 by Trigger Publishing
An imprint of Shaw Callaghan Ltd

UK Office
The Stanley Building
7 Pancras Square
Kings Cross
London N1C 4AG

US Office
On Point Executive Center, Inc
3030 N Rocky Point Drive W
Suite 150
Tampa, FL 33607
www.triggerpublishing.com

A CIP catalogue record for this book is available upon request from the British Library
ISBN: 978-1-83796-302-7
Ebook ISBN: 978-1-83796-303-4

Cover design by MoreVisual Ltd
Typeset by Lapiz Digital Services

CONTENTS

Preface: A Revolution in Psychotherapy by Shinzen Young   vii
Introduction: What Lies Beyond Talk Therapy?   xi

Part One: Unified Mindfulness   **1**
Chapter 1   Why We Suffer and How Mindfulness Helps   3
Chapter 2   What Is Unified Mindfulness?   27
Chapter 3   How to Note and Label   45
Chapter 4   Focus on Rest Technique   57
Chapter 5   Focus Out and Focus In Techniques   69
Chapter 6   Focus on Everything Technique   77
Chapter 7   Nurture the Positive   83
Chapter 8   Self-Imaging   93

Part Two: Mindfulness and Exposure Therapy –
A Fortuitous Collaboration   **101**
Chapter 9   Unified Mindfulness Exposure and
Desensitization Process – Origins
and Introduction   103
Chapter 10   The UMED Process – Six Basic Steps   129
Chapter 11   Taking the Edge Off Anxiety   157
Chapter 12   Turning Panic into Ease   169
Chapter 13   Dissolving Addictions and Other Negative
Behaviours   175
Chapter 14   Unwinding Obsessive-Compulsive Disorder
and Impulse Control Issues   193
Chapter 15   Healing Trauma   201
Chapter 16   Alternate Routes   211

Part Three: The End of All Stories   **215**

Chapter 17   Freedom Within and Beyond All Stories   217

Resources   231

Acknowledgments   235

PREFACE:
A REVOLUTION IN
PSYCHOTHERAPY

There's a revolution taking place in the world of psychotherapy. While various forms of talk therapy can be helpful for certain individuals and issues, there are broader and deeper ways in which people can be healed and empowered. What's the source of such alternatives to traditional talk therapy? It lies in the world's contemplative traditions and their psycho-spiritual practices designed to cultivate inner sensitivity, quietude, wisdom and equanimity.

Focus techniques originally derived from such contemplative traditions are now being applied to practical goals, such as relief from emotional suffering, achieving mental tranquility, changing habitual patterns – and even contacting the primordial perfection that underlies all ordinary experience.

THE BEST OF THE EAST MEETS
THE BEST OF THE WEST

An auspicious convergence of maths, imagination and empiricism gained huge momentum in Europe in the 16th and 17th centuries, giving birth to what became known as the Scientific Revolution. Western science developed the Scientific Method, which balances the power of a mathematical description with the power of mental idealization of a physical system. And in recent years the Scientific Method has been further empowered and validated in its collaboration with large-scale experimental endeavours.

When people think about the most significant scientific breakthroughs of the last century, they probably think of things like quantum mechanics and general relativity. And these have certainly been momentous achievements within the realm of physics.

However, from a practical point of view, it's possible that one of the most important discoveries of the 20th century was that meditation, mindfulness and other forms of contemplative practice could become science-aligned, science-validated and science-normalized. This mindfulness revolution was originally ignited by Jon Kabat-Zinn and his Mindfulness-Based Stress Reduction (MBSR) protocols.

Practices such as mindfulness, meditation and contemplation are often considered "Eastern" while things like clinical medicine and rigorous scientific investigation are thought of as "Western." But this is an over-simplification. Eastern cultures played a significant role in the history of science; and Western cultures have developed their own meditation traditions.

There is a rich complementarity between what the East can offer with its meditative expertise and what the West can offer with rigorous quantified science. Shelly Young's psychotherapy method brings these two together to support improved mental health in her clients.

EQUANIMITY AND EMOTIONAL INTELLIGENCE

The meditative traditions of the world (both East and West) centre on a quality that in the Unified Mindfulness system used in this book and throughout the larger mindfulness community is usually referred to as equanimity.

Developing the skill of equanimity is a fundamental aspect of self-exploration and emotional intelligence, which you'll learn a lot more about in this book. Basically, between suppression on one side and identification on the other lies a third possibility, which is a balanced state of non-self-interference in body and mind. This is equanimity.

In providing clients with training in equanimity, Shelly Young's method applies the wisdom cultivated through centuries of contemplative practice to here-and-now psychological challenges. In addition, the cognitive component of Shelly's therapeutic interventions embodies the essence of modern rationality – logic, evidence and causal reasoning. So once again, Shelly's method represents a cross-fertilization of the best practices of humanity's past with the best practices of our present.

THE SECRET SAUCE

Shelly Young's work as a science-informed and mindfulness-based psychotherapist is an inspiring example of what the recent revolution in psychotherapy is achieving.

Shelly gets results and, quite often, gets them quickly. Clients suffering from a wide range of perceptual and behavioural challenges stream into her unassuming home or online office. Despite the intensity and diversity of their difficulties, they sometimes get what they need in just a few sessions. And even when the process takes longer, it unfolds in the most intelligent and efficient possible way.

So, what's the secret? It's surprisingly simple. Shelly gives her clients *tangible focus strategies* that they can apply in the moment when things come up in their lives.

In this book, you'll learn how to implement these strategies for yourself. Explore and enjoy!

– Shinzen Young

INTRODUCTION: WHAT LIES BEYOND TALK THERAPY?

Welcome to *When Therapy Doesn't Work: A Mindfulness Guide to Emotional Repair.* Within these pages you'll find step-by-step instructions for a user-friendly and science-informed approach to a mindfulness training called Unified Mindfulness. You'll also learn how to use these mindfulness techniques to help resolve a wide variety of psychological challenges, including anxiety, panic, obsessive-compulsive disorder (OCD), addiction and trauma. I trust you'll find much of value here, and invite you to dive right in and enjoy the journey.

To begin, a few words about the origin of this book ...

FROM SHELLY YOUNG

As a psychotherapist, addiction counselor and mindfulness instructor, I've spent many years helping students and clients transform their lives by using simple focusing techniques. I have witnessed individuals with seemingly hopeless mental–emotional challenges find peace and freedom – even amid the most daunting circumstances.

Since I am myself one of those people who was able to overcome deeply entrenched and seemingly hopeless psychological obstacles, I can now share my experience and offer genuine hope for anyone who is seeking relief from the inevitable sufferings of life. My passion as a mindfulness-centred psychotherapist stems not only from my own personal transformation, but also from a deep belief in every person's ability to discover their own inherent core of peace and harmony.

MY STORY OF HOPELESSNESS TRANSFORMED

Once upon a time, I walked the colourful streets of Berkeley, California. The atmosphere was so bizarre that I was easily distracted from my agonizing feelings of self-loathing, self-pity, hopelessness, fear and despair. Here on Berkeley's Telegraph Avenue, I could forget my swollen ankles, hands and legs – swollen from the consumption of massive amounts of sugary foods and refined carbohydrates.

As I wandered this street in the 1970s, I could lose myself in its hustle and bustle and its unusual forms of creative expression, some of which seemed oddly beautiful and others downright pathological. But day after day, hour upon hour, I was utterly consumed and tormented by a sugar and food obsession. Sugar, in particular, was my perpetual nemesis and complete ruination.

Prior to the Berkeley era, I had abstained from bingeing for seven months while attending Overeaters Anonymous meetings. But when I moved to northern California, I fell off the wagon once again and gained fifty pounds in three months. Clinical depression accompanied the bingeing as I approached a nonfunctional existence. I was diagnosed with a mood disorder but refused to take the prescribed medication.

ONE PENNY

I awoke one morning and groggily opened my purse to find only one penny. That was a most memorable morning! I had a stark choice: welfare or a psychiatric hospital. I chose welfare and could barely get myself to the office to apply. Along with the welfare came food stamps – and I binged away a month's worth immediately.

If I was lucky enough to stop eating, I would start chewing. Transformed into a sorbitol junkie, I chewed twenty to thirty packs of sugarless gum per day. Chewing-gum wrappers were strewn all over my room, and I suffered from incessant bouts of daily diarrhea. Berkeley was the place where I stumbled along aimlessly from day to day, trying to make the most out of a quarter (or less).

LONGING FOR A WAY OUT

One day in 1980 I desperately searched the *Bay Guardian*, a small San Francisco newspaper. I longed for a way out of my living hell. I saw an advertisement for Zen meditation and phoned the teacher immediately. When he answered the phone, I asked, "Do you have peace of mind?" He said "Yes" in a way that was truly genuine. I made an appointment and was on his doorstep the very next day, which happened to be my 29th birthday.

Kozan Beck, a Zen teacher in the Soto tradition, opened the door. I quickly sensed a true peacefulness about him. I had met lots of people in my life who smiled a lot or who were energetic, charismatic, vivacious and friendly. But I had never met anyone with what I considered to be true peace of mind. I wanted what he had and knew I would do anything to achieve it.

MY MEDITATION JOURNEY BEGINS

On that day – February 24, 1980 – my meditation journey began. But it wouldn't be until nearly 20 years later – after practising meditation with Kozan and other teachers – that my training and work as a psychotherapist would begin in earnest.

After some additional time in Berkeley learning from Kozan, I moved to Los Angeles to study with another Zen Master. It was through this new community that I learned about and subsequently met meditation teacher Shinzen Young, who was then the vice-abbot of the International Buddhist Meditation Center.

Shinzen later founded and became the director of the Community Meditation Center of Los Angeles, and I served as its co-director. Over the coming years, I co-taught mindfulness retreats and programs with Shinzen, and then eventually began to teach on my own. It is the mindfulness techniques developed by Shinzen Young that are the focus and foundation of this book.

A NEW CAREER PATH

I went on to receive training in psychotherapy and then, in 2005, was formally licensed to practise. My motivation to embark upon this career path was twofold.

On one hand, my personal experience as a client with various forms of talk therapy had been largely disappointing; talk therapy just never worked for me. There were no deep transformations, no breakthroughs into genuine peace and harmony. It always ended up feeling like a dead end, like I was just spinning my wheels.

And on the other, the mindfulness meditation techniques that I learned from Shinzen Young and other teachers turned out to be more therapeutic than any of the more conventional therapies I had encountered.

SIMPLE AND PROFOUND HEALING

I had also noticed, with greater and greater interest, a variety of simple and profound mental and emotional healings occurring among fellow meditators – in particular, those who were applying Shinzen Young's mindfulness methods. These methods, which serve as the foundation of this book, evolved over time. The system, as a whole, became known as Basic Mindfulness and more recently as Unified Mindfulness. You'll learn much more about these methods in the coming chapters!

On numerous occasions, I witnessed firsthand the therapeutic value of mindfulness among the members of our meditation community. I saw that the practices allowed people to deeply transform themselves and I was truly inspired.

For example, one woman – who was a resident of the Community Meditation Center of Los Angeles – suffered from bulimia to such an extent that the disease was killing her. But after she consulted daily with Shinzen and applied mindfulness techniques with dedication, this challenging mental, emotional and behavioural pattern began to dissolve and, ultimately, transformed completely.

WHY I CHOSE TO BECOME A PSYCHOTHERAPIST

I decided to become a psychotherapist to give therapeutic credibility to the Unified Mindfulness system of meditation and to clearly demonstrate that therapy does not have to be a dead end (as it had been for me) – but rather can be a catalyst for both psychological healing and spiritual insight. Even when traditional forms of therapy don't work, mindfulness methods can successfully facilitate emotional repair.

For many years, I experimented with different ways of incorporating Unified Mindfulness techniques into the therapeutic process. My training in Eye Movement Desensitization and Reprocessing (EMDR) was a turning point in the evolution of my approach. I discovered the awesome power of exposure and desensitization protocols and applied this knowledge, in conjunction with mindfulness methods, to create the innovative Unified Mindfulness Exposure and Desensitization (UMED) Process, which you'll learn more about in Part Two of this book.

SOME AMAZING RESULTS

From my earliest days of practising psychotherapy, I was seeing largely positive and sometimes truly marvelous results with the clients I was working with. I always had my own unique approach to therapy – rooted in the mindfulness methods I had learned – and ended up using very little of what I had been taught in graduate school.

During my first internship at a Veteran's Center, I argued with my supervisor because he wanted me to use his psychoanalytic approach, and I wanted to employ mindfulness-based methods. I remember saying to him, with all respectful earnestness, "What I'm doing is working really well, so why would I want to do something else?"

In this conversation, I was referring to my very first client, who was a Vietnam veteran suffering from post-traumatic stress disorder (PTSD). The results of his man's treatment, using the mindfulness methods, were outstanding – and I presented his case for the completion of my Master's degree.

I ended up leaving that internship and found another one where my therapeutic approach was fully accepted. In fact, my new supervisor became very interested in Shinzen Young's Unified Mindfulness system and went on to study his work in depth.

WHY I DECIDED TO WRITE THIS BOOK

Years later, while sitting one day in my Albuquerque office, I felt a strong desire welling up – to find a way to share more widely the always inspiring and occasionally miraculous results of this mindfulness-centred way of doing therapy. By that time, I had worked with hundreds of clients and witnessed both ordinary and breathtaking transformations of seemingly hopeless situations.

I knew that it was no longer okay to keep this all to myself like a prized personal treasure. I needed to spread the wealth – to get these methods out there, so that more people could learn about and benefit from them. I wanted to let others know about the powerful applications of Unified Mindfulness in both psychotherapy and as a self-help tool that can easily be applied to all of life's myriad circumstances. And so, I made the decision to write this book and invited Elizabeth Reninger to assist with this project.

FROM ELIZABETH RENINGER

When I first met Shelly Young, it was in a context completely unrelated to mindfulness training or psychotherapy – just one of those wonderfully serendipitous crossings of paths, when life brings us exactly what we most need in the moment. I had recently injured my back, so was moving about quite gingerly as we introduced ourselves. Noticing my discomfort, Shelly offered to teach me a mindfulness technique, which she said might alleviate some of the pain or at least dissolve the psychological resistance to it. What a beautiful, warmhearted gesture this was, this willingness to be of service to a complete stranger, and I was touched by the kind generosity and sweetness of it.

The method Shelly suggested was a simple one. "Just find a place in your body," she said, "that *does* feel comfortable, and gently rest your attention at that place, simply noticing and enjoying the comfort." After several minutes of doing this, I did indeed feel better. Though I could still feel a bit of pain in my back, my mental and emotional relationship to those sensations had shifted dramatically. I felt more spacious, more at ease with the situation.

In the years following this initial encounter, Shelly and I ended up becoming good friends. And it was through this connection that I learned about Shinzen Young, the man whose system of mindfulness training had been the basis of the practice Shelly offered to me that day, when I was schlepping around with a tweaked back.

I attended several of Shinzen's residential retreats and for a couple of years participated regularly in his tele-seminar Home Practice Program. I enjoyed this form of practice and appreciated the mental and emotional clarification and insight it facilitated.

So, when Shelly invited me to be part of this project – writing a book that applies Shinzen's mindfulness techniques to a psychotherapeutic context – my answer was an easy yes. I was happy to do my part in making these beneficial practices more widely available.

Shinzen revels in the conversation between contemplative practice and Western science, and his Unified Mindfulness system is deeply rooted in this intersection of objective and subjective explorations. This is perfect for those whose confidence in the practice of mindfulness is enhanced by knowing that it has been validated via the methods of Western science. Whether or not one shares this passion for the science–spirit interface, the techniques themselves can be deeply effective.

Among the multitude of methods offered by Shinzen's Unified Mindfulness system, it's easy to find at least one with which we resonate, one that feels useful or interesting. In developing her UMED Process, Shelly has chosen to emphasize just five or six of these methods, in a way that has brought great benefit to many.

I trust that those who are drawn to read this book will, in a similar fashion, benefit by coming to understand more clearly how the suffering associated with our "me-story" is created and how this suffering can be fully dissolved, leaving us free to create new stories and to dance and play in the space prior to and beyond all stories.

My role in this wonderful project has been to assist with the writing. Please note, however, that the primary narrator throughout the book is Shelly Young. Except for a few sections (mostly in Chapters 2 and 3) that are explicitly attributed to Shinzen Young, the "I" is the voice of Shelly, introducing you to powerful Unified Mindfulness methods for supporting emotional repair.

* * *

WHAT IS MINDFULNESS TRAINING?

"Men go abroad to wonder at the heights of mountains, at the huge waves of the sea, at the long courses of the rivers, at the vast compass of the ocean, at the circular motion of the stars; and they pass by themselves without wondering."

Saint Augustine

What exactly is mindfulness training? You'll learn quite a bit about this over the course of the book ... but, for starters, we can say that mindfulness training will support you in cultivating a healthy, strong and flexible mind – in much the same way as cardio and weight training help build a healthy, strong and flexible body.

These mindfulness methods have the power to deeply transform the mental, emotional and behavioural patterns – the old stories – that you may currently feel trapped or oppressed by. They have the power to unwind the suffering associated with these habitual patterns in a way that may be much more effective than anything you've tried so far, including more traditional forms of counseling or psychotherapy. They can serve as your guide to emotional repair. Best of all, these methods are designed to unveil deep comfort and ease, causeless joy and true freedom. They are strong medicine and they're here for you now.

The techniques you'll learn in the upcoming chapters can be applied to your own circumstances and your own psychological issues. They can also be shared with friends or family members. And if you're a healing professional, mindfulness tools can easily be incorporated into your current therapeutic protocols or used as a standalone technique.

IS THIS BOOK FOR YOU?

You might be wondering, *Is this book a good one for me?* Well, you're very likely to benefit from what's offered here if:

1. You've tried conventional counseling or talk therapy and it hasn't worked.
2. You've practised mindfulness and want to learn how to apply it more directly to specific mental–emotional challenges.
3. You are brand new to mindfulness and want to learn the basics.
4. You're a mental health professional eager to incorporate mindfulness techniques into your work with clients.

If any of these is true of you, then this book is for you!

HOW TO USE THIS BOOK

You can read this book straight through, from start to finish. Alternatively, you can focus on just one of its three main parts – each of which delivers unique benefits.

- **Read the Introduction** for some basic definitions; a general overview of the relationship between psychotherapy, mental health and mindfulness; and a summary of the scientific validation and overall benefits of mindfulness.
- **Use Part One** to learn the basic reasons why we suffer and how mindfulness can provide relief from psychological suffering. In Part One you'll also learn some specific Unified Mindfulness techniques to get you started. If you're new to mindfulness, you'll need to read these before moving on to the therapeutic applications discussed in Part Two.
- **Use Part Two** to learn about my unique protocol – the Unified Mindfulness Exposure and Desensitization (UMED)

Process – for applying Unified Mindfulness techniques to emotional repair; and using it to effectively transform specific psychological conditions such as anxiety, panic, trauma, OCD and addictions.

Whichever route you choose through the book, be sure to **finish with Part Three** – which offers a glimpse of the ordinary and extraordinary levels of wellbeing and fulfillment that can be enjoyed once the root-cause of psychological suffering is fully comprehended and emotional repair has been deeply engaged with.

SOME BASIC DEFINITIONS

Let's start with some basic definitions, so we have a shared language for what follows. This will make it easier for you to navigate – with comfort, ease and confidence – the mindfulness exercises that will be introduced in Part One and the therapeutic protocols of Part Two. This is how Shinzen Young – the founder of Unified Mindfulness – uses these terms, and I will be using them in the same way.

MINDFULNESS (OR MINDFUL AWARENESS)
Mindfulness – also sometimes referred to here as "mindful awareness" – is a certain way to pay attention to what is happening around you and within you. It also refers to a set of skills you can cultivate to strengthen and refine your attention.

More specifically, mindfulness encompasses three attention skills – concentration power, sensory clarity and equanimity – all working together:

1. **Concentration** is the ability to focus on what you deem to be relevant.

2. **Clarity** is the ability to detect and untangle the strands of your experience.
3. **Equanimity** is a kind of inner balance that represents a third possibility between pushing sensory experience down (suppressing) and being pulled away by the sensory experience (grasping).

MINDFULNESS TECHNIQUES OR METHODS

Mindfulness techniques or methods are specific focus exercises that are designed to elevate your base level of concentration power, sensory clarity and equanimity. Shinzen Young's Unified Mindfulness system includes 16 core techniques – 16 different methods for cultivating concentration, clarity and equanimity. In this book, you'll be learning some of these foundational core methods.

Specifically, the Unified Mindfulness techniques that you'll be learning in Part One of this book include: Focus on Rest, Focus Out, Focus In, Focus on Everything, Nurture the Positive and Self-Imaging.

NOTING AND LABELING

One way to develop mindful awareness is by clearly acknowledging the existence of sensory experiences (for example, sights, sounds, feelings) and then gently, intently focusing on them, for a short amount of time. This gentle yet vivid focusing is called **noting**.

Labeling is an option that can be used in conjunction with noting. Labels are mental or spoken words that name the specific sensory experience you are focusing on (aka "noting") at that moment.

More detailed instruction on how to note and label – while engaging in mindfulness exercises – will be provided in Part One. For now, it's enough to understand that noting and labeling are key components of a mindfulness practice.

UNIFIED MINDFULNESS AND ULTRA

Shinzen Young's approach to mindfulness training is encompassed by two interrelated systems: Unified Mindfulness and ULTRA.

Unified Mindfulness is Shinzen's system of science-informed mindfulness training that integrates insights and practices from contemplative traditions around the world.

ULTRA – the Universal Library for Training Attention – arranges all the world's focus techniques into four basic themes which describe the fields of application and profound benefits of mindfulness practice. These themes are:

1. Appreciate self and world
2. Transcend self and world
3. Nurture positivity and
4. Express spontaneity

UNIFIED MINDFULNESS EXPOSURE AND DESENSITIZATION PROCESS

The **Unified Mindfulness Exposure and Desensitization (UMED) Process** is a blending of psychotherapeutic principles with the Unified Mindfulness system developed by Shinzen Young. It is my application of Shinzen Young's Unified Mindfulness techniques to emotional repair and psychological transformation. The UMED Process interweaves exposure and desensitization protocols and cognitive behavioural techniques with mindfulness methods to support deep healing while at the same time facilitating insight into the root cause of psychological suffering; and opening the way to lasting peace and freedom.

Don't worry if this seems like a lot of information! Remember that you can bookmark this page and refer to it whenever you need. Eventually you'll become familiar with and comfortable using these terms.

WHY THERAPY SOMETIMES DOESN'T WORK

There are dozens if not hundreds of different types of counseling and psychotherapy (aka talk therapy). What these various psychological healing modalities have in common is their intention to help people identify and change troubling thoughts, emotions and/or behaviours.

Traditional forms of talk therapy can sometimes be helpful for certain people and issues. They can provide a venue for an individual to express themselves, to receive support in sorting things out and perhaps gain some genuine insight into their troubling emotions or problematic behaviours.

But sometimes therapy doesn't work. The issues that a person seeks to resolve are not resolved – even after months or years of regular sessions. So, why do traditional therapies sometimes not work to transform behaviour and facilitate emotional repair on their own? There are many possible reasons, including:

- The specific psychotherapeutic modality might not be the most effective one for a given person.
- The relationship between the client and the therapist may not elicit the comfort and trust required for deep transformation.
- The client may be unable or unwilling to follow through consistently with the suggestions made by the therapist.

These are just some of the reasons why traditional talk therapy may come up short – may fail to deliver the emotional repair and deep transformation that is most needed.

The good news is that there are broader and deeper ways in which people can be healed and empowered – and mindfulness-centred psychotherapy is one of these. Many forms of traditional talk therapy have radically different assumptions and approaches than a mindfulness practice. However, sometimes the two can work very well together.

HOW PSYCHOTHERAPY AND MINDFULNESS CAN WORK TOGETHER

While psychotherapy on its own sometimes doesn't work, mindfulness and certain types of therapy can complement each other beautifully. My Unified Mindfulness Exposure and Desensitization (UMED) Process is one example of this fruitful collaboration.

Both psychotherapy and mindfulness practice are about understanding ourselves more clearly, reducing emotional suffering, connecting with genuine sources of nourishment and cultivating a wise and loving presence. Both practices aim to enhance our relationship with ourselves and with others, so that our thoughts, words and actions become more easeful, balanced and harmonious.

The healing process facilitated by psychotherapy requires focus, commitment and resilience – which a mindfulness practice helps to cultivate. The concentration, clarity and equanimity that are developed via mindfulness exercises can enhance the effectiveness of whatever other therapeutic modalities we happen to be engaged in.

A mindfulness practice can also nurture a more precise and comfortable relationship with the physical sensations in our body which, in turn, can help us learn how to effectively regulate our nervous system. This is a key aspect of the healing process, especially for trauma survivors and people suffering from post-traumatic stress disorder (PTSD).

Both therapy and mindfulness encourage a vibrant, curious and caring attention to every aspect of our human experience, whether it's something that we are seeing or hearing, or the felt sensations of the breath in our body or the mind's inner dialogue. Over time, both therapy and a mindfulness practice can help us cultivate a deeper understanding of ourselves and a more kind, courageous and fulfilling way of inhabiting our world.

In addition – and perhaps most importantly – both therapy and mindfulness practice encourage us to step back from a compulsively speedy "doing" mode, and instead cultivate the ability to stop, settle and simply be. It's only then that we can authentically encounter, embrace, explore and transform our suffering – and most fully enjoy our human existence.

THE UNIQUE POWER OF MINDFULNESS-CENTRED THERAPY

What makes mindfulness-centred therapy uniquely powerful?

Mindfulness-based therapy is about making friends with thoughts and feelings. It's about releasing the compulsive fight – the agitation, constriction, shaming and blaming – within yourself. It's about cultivating a genuinely kind, intelligently discerning and nonjudgmental way of relating to yourself. It's an "acceptance strategy" much more than it is a "change strategy."

This doesn't mean that change doesn't happen. On the contrary, deep transformations are a common occurrence in mindfulness-centred therapy. But such changes tend to arise naturally, organically, spontaneously, out of the "place" of radical acceptance. They emerge from the deep wisdom that an attitude of welcoming and equanimity puts you in touch with. Mindfulness techniques skillfully applied within the field of welcoming are what make profound healing possible.

THE GOAL OF MINDFULNESS-CENTRED THERAPY

The overall goal of my mindfulness-centred psychotherapy practice, as I work with individual clients, is twofold: to decrease suffering and to enhance fulfillment and wellbeing. This twofold intention sometimes entails behavioural change – releasing negative behaviours and adding more positive habits and beneficial routines to a person's life. It can also include helping a client decrease their level of suffering around thoughts and feelings that are rooted in specific belief systems by explicitly challenging and learning to let go of negative beliefs and replacing them with more empowering ones.

Central to each of these aspirations is training in equanimity – one of the key components (along with concentration and clarity) of mindful awareness.

EQUANIMITY, SUFFERING AND FULFILLMENT

Equanimity – which you'll learn a lot more about in upcoming chapters – is a fundamental skill for self-exploration and emotional intelligence. Shinzen defines it as "a balanced state of non-interference in body and in mind that avoids the extremes of suppression and identification." Suppression and identification are imbalanced states that are rooted in ignorance and fuel psychological suffering.

1. **Suppression** is when an internal or external sensory experience arises and we attempt to cope with it by denying it, tightening around it, pushing it away, stuffing it down, etc.
2. **Identification** is when an internal or external sensory experience arises and we grasp or fixate on it, holding

onto it inappropriately and not letting it arise, transform and pass away in its own natural rhythm.

Between suppression on one side and identification on the other lies the third possibility of equanimity – where sensory experience flows naturally, effortlessly and with great vividness.

When my clients train in equanimity, they learn to experience thoughts, feelings and sensations passing through the field of their awareness like clouds drifting through a vast blue sky. They learn to relate to them with spacious intimacy, benevolent indifference and/or friendly curiosity.

They also learn this vitally important lesson – that with equanimity, discomfort (painful sensations) causes them less psychological suffering; and pleasure (pleasant sensations) brings more fulfillment. In this way, the equanimity component of mindfulness has the power to both decrease suffering and enhance fulfillment.

EQUANIMITY AND RESPONSE-ABILITY

Paradoxically, internal equanimity/passivity can enhance a client's response-ability – their capacity to act externally in ways that are most appropriate to the situation. In other words, internal equanimity doesn't imply external passivity. On the contrary, it can dramatically increase the effectiveness of external activity.

Imagine, for example, that your young child has run out into a busy street, causing several cars to come screeching to a halt to avoid hitting them. If you have cultivated equanimity via mindfulness practice, you'll be able to fully welcome whatever emotions arise in that moment – surprise, anxiety, panic, anger and so on – without being immobilized or crippled by these emotions. Instead, you'll move quickly and efficiently to bring your child safely away from the street and then lovingly explain to them why it's best to stay in the yard and away from traffic. So, you can be fully mindful and internally passive – in the sense of residing in equanimity – while simultaneously being decisive in taking external action.

SENSORY EXPERIENCE IN THE HERE AND NOW

Mindfulness happens only in the here and now. It's about how you relate to experiences such as seeing, hearing, feeling and internal thoughts/images – *in this very moment*. A mindfulness-centred therapy is less interested in exploring narratives of past events or thinking ahead into the future. Its primary interest – and the source of its unique power – is in attending with mindful awareness to what is happening here and now.

Our here-and-now human experience has three fundamental aspects, each of which can be attended to mindfully. These three realms of experience are:

1. **An Internal World** that consists of thoughts (internal dialogue), mental images and feelings (emotional sensations). In terms of emotional repair, we're especially interested in this aspect of human experience – thoughts, mental images and feelings – since it is within these realms that psychological suffering arises.
2. **An External World** that is accessed via our human sense organs: our eyes, ears, nose, tongue and skin. So, this external world – as we experience it – consists of sights, sounds, tastes, smells and tactile sensations.
3. **Periods of Rest** that are characterized by the *absence* of internal or external sensory experience. For example, each time you close your eyes, you experience a kind of "visual

rest" with the *absence* of external visual phenomena. And no matter how speedy your mental self-talk may be, there are (if you look closely) at least micro-moments of internal silence: the absence of thinking.

SUFFERING AND FREEDOM

And here's the key point in relation to psychological suffering and the fundamental components of human experience:

Without exception, all forms of suffering – and all mental health issues – involve some combination of seeing, hearing and feeling. In other words, all psychological disturbances are comprised of the same basic threads of sensory experience. All involve patterns of internal and/or external images, sounds/ internal dialogue, physical sensations and emotional feelings.

So, how we *relate to* these aspects of our human experience determines whether we experience psychological suffering or freedom. When we're heavily identified with, feeling swept away or overwhelmed by our thoughts, emotions or physical sensations, then we experience psychological suffering.

When these strands of experience are constricted or entangled, suffering ensues. As these strands of experience are untangled – say, via a mindfulness practice – then deep healing, a sense of wellbeing, lasting peace and unconditioned joy emerge. This is the unique power of mindfulness-centred therapy.

SENSORY CLARITY: DISENTANGLE AND BE FREE

The Unified Mindfulness system emphasizes your relationship with (both internal and external) seeing, hearing and feeling –

and changing that relationship in ways that decrease suffering and elevate fulfillment.

You may recall that mindfulness has three main components: concentration power, sensory clarity and equanimity. The second of these – sensory clarity – is all about clarifying and beneficially transforming your relationship to the content of your human experience – for example, to what, in any given moment, you are seeing, hearing or feeling; or the mental chatter and internal images arising and dissolving in your mind.

With the mindfulness methods presented in this book, you'll be training your mind and even changing your brain in deeply beneficial ways. You'll learn to avoid "locking onto" or "collapsing into" thoughts and feelings – which causes suffering. Instead, you'll allow them to do their dance and then pass right through.

Instead of being like solid icebergs in your heart and mind, thoughts and feelings will become as fluid as flowing stream-water. And the mental health challenges frozen into those icebergs will also begin to melt and flow and, perhaps, even dissolve completely.

AN INSPIRING CASE STUDY: FROM ANGER TO CONTENTMENT

Here's just one example of a client for whom traditional therapy didn't work, but who experienced deep healing and transformation with my mindfulness-based approach.

Ellie presented with post-traumatic stress disorder (PTSD) resulting from her marriage to a man with narcissistic personality disorder. She had been to several traditional talk therapists with no success and was extremely skeptical about therapy working for her.

Her main symptoms were constant extreme anger and agitating thoughts that continued almost nonstop throughout the day.

In my therapeutic work with her, I taught Ellie the Focus Out mindfulness technique to help her feel more grounded. Then, as she calmed down, I added the Focus on Everything technique to help her cultivate moment-by-moment sensory clarity. (You'll learn more about these mindfulness methods in Part One.) We also worked with exposure and desensitization protocols (more on this in Part Two) using, as a trigger, the image of her former husband and his most disturbing actions.

Ellie was very devoted to and consistent in practising the methods and gradually began to feel better. She employed the mindfulness techniques on-and-off throughout the day, especially when thoughts of her former husband would arise. As a result, the anger and disturbing thoughts began to dissipate; she became more comfortable, calm and poised and her nervous system regained a healthy balance between its sympathetic (fight-flight-freeze) and parasympathetic (rest-digest-restore) functions.

Within a few months Ellie left therapy feeling genuinely happy and content. The emotional repair that traditional therapies failed to deliver had been successfully completed via my mindfulness-centred approach.

The power of working directly with strands of sensory experience (thoughts, images and feelings) via a mindfulness method lies in its ability to take an overwhelmingly disturbing emotional reaction and divide it up into manageable "pieces." This is the superpower inherent in the sensory clarity component of mindfulness.

So, in Ellie's case, instead of running the story, "My husband is horrible and I hate him, and he did these terrible things to me," she employed the mindfulness method labels, *see* (for internal images), *hear* (for mental dialogue) and *feel* (for physical or emotional sensations). This simple tool extricated her from the entangled storyline and returned her attention to here-and-now, moment-by-moment sensory experience. It put her in touch with reality as it *is* rather than as she was imagining (hoping and/or fearing) it to be.

RELEASING THE STORY

A saying I often share with my clients is: "Suffering is always decreased when the story is released." Stories – the complex narratives constructed and repeated in your mind – are typically infused with emotional reactivity. So, latching onto the story tends to fuel the fire of psychological suffering.

Unified Mindfulness methods help you divide both the story and your emotional reactivity up into smaller segments – so they lose their power to seduce, constrict and control your body and/or mind, and to veil your natural peace and freedom.

Over time, such a mindfulness practice (with noting and labeling) creates long-lasting positive changes. Your equanimity in relation to thoughts and feelings becomes more effortless and spontaneous. Thoughts and feelings, as they arise, just naturally pass right through, without congealing into patterns that cause psychological suffering.

You may have heard of archetypes – images, patterns or character-types that symbolize something universal in our human experience. If you're inspired by the warrior archetype, you can think of this process of dividing an emotional reaction into smaller segments as a *divide-and-conquer* strategy for winning the war against ignorance and suffering. If you resonate more easily with artists, alchemists, detectives or chess masters, you might describe it instead as a *disentangle-and-be-free* game-plan. In either case, mindfulness-centred therapy is a powerful tool for emotional repair!

THE UMED PROCESS AND EMDR

One of the traditional psychological tools that my UMED Process employs is called "exposure and desensitization." You'll learn a lot more about this in Part Two. For now, I just want to acknowledge my use of this tool and also be clear about how its use within the UMED Process differs from how it is employed within Eye Movement Desensitization and Reprocessing (EMDR).

Francine Shapiro – the creator of EMDR – brilliantly demonstrated the therapeutic potency of exposure and desensitization. And her work has provided a powerful framework for my UMED Process.

While the UMED Process utilizes exposure and desensitization protocols rooted in EMDR, there are some significant differences between EMDR and the UMED Process that are worth noting here:

1. The UMED Process does not use bilateral stimulation of any kind. I have found the mindfulness techniques themselves to be sufficient in facilitating desensitization, deep healing and transformation. (You can read more about my decision to employ mindfulness techniques along with and then in place of bilateral stimulation in Chapter 9.)

2. The UMED Process does not use a "safe place" – having the client imagine a person, place or thing associated with safety and protection that they "go to" internally when feeling unsafe. Instead, in therapeutic settings, UMED clients are trained in Unified Mindfulness techniques before they engage in any exposure and desensitization process. They are fully grounded in the application of such methods for emotional regulation and must demonstrate adequate mental and emotional stability before the therapist begins any exposure and desensitization

efforts. The Unified Mindfulness techniques themselves then become the "go to" for resolving any emotional disturbances that may occur during treatment.

3. Like EMDR, the UMED Process instructs the client to practise saying "no" to one or more negative beliefs by "installing" a positive belief. However, the mindfulness-centred therapist augments this method with the Unified Mindfulness Nurture the Positive technique. This supplies a powerful means of saying "yes" to a positive belief, as well as positive, empowering actions, and has proven to be greatly transformative and uplifting for therapy clients.

MINDFULNESS AND WESTERN SCIENCE

People have been practising mindfulness for thousands of years as an aspect of both Eastern and Western spiritual traditions and – more recently – in various secular contexts.

Each person who has practised mindfulness has had their own subjective experience of its results. Over time, they've noticed changes that they attribute to their mindfulness practice. In other words, mindfulness has been subjectively validated via countless practitioners themselves, over millennia. As the well-known adage goes: "The proof of the pudding is in the eating." The true value of mindfulness is in how it beneficially transforms our own life-experience.

It's only more recently that western scientists have had the tools (rooted in the Scientific Method) and have become interested in providing objective verification of the physical, mental and/or emotional benefits of mindfulness practice. Starting in the 1960s – and particularly since the 1980s – there have been increasing numbers of rigorous peer-reviewed scientific studies that have demonstrated the effectiveness of mindfulness training.

At the time of writing this book there are literally tens of thousands of such studies. According to the US National Institute on Health, from 1966 to 2021 there were 16,581 publications on mindfulness research[*]!

Through well-controlled scientific trials, the effectiveness of mindfulness training in **1) reducing distress** and **2) increasing quality of life** (which correspond to my two main goals in working with clients) has been convincingly demonstrated. There's lots to explore, for those of you who are interested in the scientific validation of mindfulness training. While such studies are not the focus of this book, it's worth noting that the most-commonly studied forms of mindfulness training, to date, are:

1. Jon Kabat-Zinn's mindfulness-based stress reduction (MBSR) and mindfulness-based cognitive therapy (MBCT).
2. Other offshoots of cognitive behavioural therapy (CBT) including Steven Hayes' acceptance and commitment therapy (ACT) and Marsha Linehan's dialectical behaviour therapy (DBT).
3. The mindfulness training developed by social psychologist Dr Ellen Langer.

RESEARCH RELATED TO THE UNIFIED MINDFULNESS SYSTEM

Shinzen Young's Unified Mindfulness system – the source of the mindfulness methods presented in this book – is known for its clarity and precision, which makes it an excellent choice for

---

[*] Baminiwatta A, Solangaarachchi I, Trends and Developments in Mindfulness Research over 55 Years: A Bibliometric Analysis of Publications Indexed in Web of Science. *Mindfulness* (N Y). 2021;12(9):2099-2116. doi: 10.1007/s12671-021-01681-x. Epub 2021 Jul 16. PMID: 34306245; PMCID: PMC8282773.

rigorous scientific studies. It is currently being used in major research projects on mindfulness and meditation at a variety of research institutions including Harvard Medical School, Carnegie Mellon University, the University of Vermont and the University of Arizona's Science Enhanced Mindful Awareness (SEMA) Laboratory.

At the SEMA Laboratory, Shinzen and his colleagues Jay Sanguinetti (SEMA Lab), Judson Brewer (Brown University Mindfulness Center), and David Creswell (Neuroscience Institute at Carnegie Mellon University) have been exploring ways of enhancing the experience of equanimity through biomodulation. Their hypothesis is that such forms of non-invasive biomodulation may help activate ancient evolutionary networks within the brain that are related to the biological origins of equanimity.

The specific form of biomodulation that they have been experimenting with is medical ultrasound. This type of ultrasound uses sound waves to penetrate soft tissues – in this case, certain tissues within the brain. What these researchers have found so far is that by affecting specific tissues in the brain, medical ultrasound can safely and reliably accelerate the acquisition of what Shinzen refers to as "sensory conductivity" – which corresponds to the equanimity component of mindfulness. (You'll learn much more about equanimity in the coming chapters.)

Enhancing the experience of equanimity in this way makes it easier for people who are just beginning to meditate to feel inspired to continue to practise. It provides a tangible reward – a "taste" of one of the sweetest outcomes of a consistent practice – to motivate them to keep going. This enhanced experience of equanimity directly supports the cultivation of concentration and clarity. Since concentration, clarity and equanimity are the three main components of mindfulness, this form of biomodulation has a direct connection to mindfulness training.

The specific regions of the brain that are being targeted by the therapeutic ultrasound include 1) the posterior cingulate cortex (PCC) – the upper part of the limbic lobe, and 2) the bilateral tip of the caudate nucleus – part of the basal ganglia. Another promising possibility is targeting the amygdala – a part of the limbic system that is involved in processing emotions, especially fear and anxiety. (You'll learn more about the amygdala in Chapter 9.)

The overall aspiration of this research is to make meditation and mindfulness training available to a greater number of people by providing a way to jumpstart the process via this type of biomodulation.

RESEARCH INVOLVING
MY UMED PROCESS

I am currently working with clinical laboratories at the University of Arizona and the Medical University of South Carolina to combine my therapeutic interventions with transcranial direct current stimulation (tCDS) and transcranial focused ultrasound (tFUS). As mentioned above, some scientists have hypothesized that these types of biomodulation have the potential to activate evolutionary networks within the brain that are related to the biological origins of equanimity. This biomodulation version of my work is currently investigational but will likely be available to the public within the next several years.

And keep an eye out also for my conversational artificial intelligence (AI) app – which is currently in its developmental stages – for supporting the transformation of addictions and negative behaviour patterns and enhancing mental health via mindfulness protocols.

BENEFITS OF MINDFULNESS PRACTICE

As mentioned above, an impressively wide array of scientific studies has established that a consistent mindfulness practice reliably leads to a reduction of mental–emotional distress and an increased quality of life. In other words, mindfulness reduces suffering and enhances wellbeing. This has been experienced directly by countless practitioners across various cultures and millennia, and has been validated by western scientists.

Shinzen Young has formulated the global benefits of a systematic mindfulness practice as bringing about five broad, long-term effects, which are:

- **Relief** – minimizing suffering
- **Satisfaction** – maximizing fulfillment
- **Wisdom** – understanding yourself at all levels
- **Mastery** – acting skillfully
- **Service** – helping from love

If this sounds pretty good to you, then read on! The mindfulness methods introduced in Part One will put you on a path to reaping similar benefits.

STRONG MEDICINE: THE UMED PROCESS

UMED – The mindfulness-centred therapeutic system that I've developed – is deeply effective and easy to learn. You'll see it in action and learn a lot more about it in Part Two of this book. In short, the UMED Process is a blending of psychotherapeutic principles with the Unified Mindfulness system developed by Shinzen Young.

Here I'll offer a glimpse of some of the inspiring transformations that I've witnessed while using this therapeutic process. All of the Unified Mindfulness techniques mentioned in these descriptions are presented in detail in Part One. In other words, you'll soon be able to use them yourself.

Jim
Having been hospitalized three times the week before for severe panic attacks, Jim came to therapy. I taught him the Unified Mindfulness Focus Out technique and, after four sessions, he was done with therapy – with no additional hospitalizations.

Stephen
Stephen – a young man in his 20s – came to therapy for anger management. He identified the root cause of the anger he was feeling as being verbal abuse that he had suffered in his childhood. After three sessions using Unified Mindfulness techniques, Stephen felt happy with his progress and empowered to continue on his own.

Pete
Pete had an elevator phobia. After just three sessions of mindfulness-centred work, he was riding the elevator alone without problems.

Sophia
Sophia was a middle-aged woman who came to therapy aspiring to quit a life-long smoking habit. After five sessions of mindfulness-centred work, she achieved this goal.

Patricia
Patricia had a decades-long habit of picking at her fingers. Her fingers were always torn and bloody, and the habit was interfering with her life in serious ways. She had tried taking

medication, but to no avail. After three sessions of the UMED Process, the pattern fully resolved and she ended therapy.

Rochelle

Rochelle came to therapy because of marital discord. After using mindfulness techniques to explore her feelings about the relationship and to become clear about her options and aspirations, she decided – from a place of clarity and empowerment – to file for a divorce.

Joanne

Joanne had been in therapy with me for a number of months. She came to a particular session experiencing severe anxiety, triggered by a recent crash in the stock market. She feared that she would not have enough money to retire. We processed the issue using the UMED Process. The issue was fully resolved after one session.

Shaun

Shaun was himself a therapist. He entered therapy (with me) to resolve his lack of self-confidence when doing therapy with his own clients. He accomplished his confidence goal in 12 sessions of mindfulness-centred work.

John

John came to my office with a single complaint, which was that he had recently been experiencing erectile dysfunction. The problem had begun after one time of (in his words) "failing to perform" sexually with his wife. He reported that, since that time, he had felt anxious about making love with her. I taught him the Focus Out technique and instructed him to practise it before and during lovemaking with his wife. He returned a few weeks later stating that he was cured and didn't require additional therapy sessions for this issue.

Jenny

Jenny was an author who came to therapy to resolve a writer's block that was manifesting as conflict around whether or not she should finish a book she had begun. With the support of Unified Mindfulness techniques, Jenny came to see clearly that she was afraid of disapproval, which was what had been preventing her from finishing the book. After five sessions, the issue fully resolved and she felt confident in her capacity to complete the project.

Jane

Jane suffered from trichotillomania – compulsive hair pulling. The issue was fully resolved, with a complete cessation of the hair-pulling behaviour and the therapy concluded after only three sessions of mindfulness-centred work.

Sonia

Sonia came to me with obsessive-compulsive disorder (OCD), manifesting as an overwhelming fear of hurting herself and others. The main "other" was her six-year-old son. Whenever she cut his nails, she became terrified that she was going to intentionally hurt him with the nail clipper. After three sessions, she felt that she no longer needed therapy for this issue.

Dina

Dina suffered from what is called "white-coat hypertension": anxiety, heart palpitations and increased blood pressure when she was in a hospital or a medical environment, or when she was using a medical device. She was most concerned about not being able to use her BEMER (Bio-Electro-Magnetic Energy Regulation device), for which she had paid many thousands of dollars. She had hoped to use this device to improve her sleep and other health issues. But whenever she lay on the mat to use her BEMER, she felt so anxious that her heart rate would skyrocket that she needed to get up immediately. After just three sessions of therapy – one of which included the UMED Process – she happily reported that she was able to use her BEMER with no problem ("I'm cured!" were her thrilled words); she did not need to continue therapy.

Carlie

Carlie suffered so severely from agoraphobia – a fear of public places – that she couldn't remember the last time she had been out of her house alone. Within a few mindfulness-based sessions, she was able to go out of the house; and after eight sessions, she went to the shopping mall alone. She was so happy to be able to go to the mall without being accompanied by her teenage daughters.

Ryan

Ryan came to my group therapy with one issue he really wanted to resolve: whenever he took a walk, he noticed his mind filling with negativity – with a barrage of toxic thoughts and emotions. I taught him how to practise the Unified Mindfulness Nurture the Positive technique and encouraged him to apply it during his walks. After a few sessions, Ryan reported complete relief from that persistent negativity. He was now enjoying many more positive and uplifting thoughts and emotions during his walks and throughout the day.

Perhaps you recognize yourself – or a friend, family member or client – in one of these descriptions. If so, please understand that there is indeed hope for the situation to transform.

As you continue to read, you'll learn a bit more about the origins of this mindfulness-centred therapy, and a lot more about how to apply it in your own personal and/or professional life.

BEFORE YOU BEGIN ...

As you make your way through the rest of this book, it will help you to keep the following points in mind.

YES, THERE IS HOPE

Anxiety, panic, OCD, addictions and trauma challenge a great many people. The good news is that there are ways to dissolve the suffering associated with these conditions – including the mindfulness methods you'll learn here.

YES, MINDFULNESS TRAINING *IS* FOR YOU

The benefits of mindfulness are available to everyone, regardless of age, health, gender, race, religious affiliation (or lack thereof) or level of education. All that's required is genuine interest.

EVERYTHING YOU NEED IS ALREADY WITHIN YOU

Mindfulness practice doesn't require any extra equipment. Your precious human mind–body is both the territory you will explore and the observational tool you will use.

ALL ARE WELCOME

Mindfulness is not about rejecting thoughts, emotions or any other aspect of your life. Instead, you'll learn how to relate to these experiences with greater clarity, acceptance and genuine intimacy – rather than becoming entangled in them.

LIVE THE EXPERIENCE INSTEAD OF THINKING IT

Like the taste of a peach, the fruits of a mindfulness practice are wholly experiential: truly known only by you. The guidance here is offered like a ripe peach in the hand of a friend: it is yours now to accept, taste and enjoy deeply.

HAVE FUN!

Think of mindfulness practices as play more than work. Trust that there is much of value to discover and take a childlike approach: be endlessly curious and open to adventure.

Bon voyage!

PART ONE

UNIFIED MINDFULNESS

Now it's time to begin your own mindfulness journey, in earnest. The first step – covered in **Chapter 1** – is to get crystal-clear on the root-cause of psychological suffering. This chapter also provides a detailed introduction to mindfulness and why it is such an effective antidote to suffering.

In **Chapter 2** you'll learn about a specific system of mindfulness practice, created by Shinzen Young, called Unified Mindfulness. This system is rooted in the essential unity of the world's contemplative traditions – what they have in common in relation to mindfulness. You'll also be treated to some of Shinzen's own thoughts on the similarities and differences between mindfulness training and therapy – how mindfulness methods can work on their own or in conjunction with psychological therapies to facilitate emotional repair.

Chapter 3 introduces noting and labeling: the nuts-and-bolts of mindfulness methods. Here you'll be guided through the basics step-by-step along with some of the more subtle points of noting and labeling various strands of your human sensory experience – which enhances the concentration, clarity and equanimity components of mindfulness.

In **Chapters 4–8** you'll have the opportunity to learn some specific Unified Mindfulness techniques – to really get your feet wet! The specific Unified Mindfulness techniques introduced in these chapters are: Focus on Rest (including Absolute Rest),

Focus Out and Focus In, Focus on Everything and Nurture the Positive. The Self-Imaging technique is a powerfully creative variation of Nurture the Positive. These six Unified Mindfulness methods form the foundation of my UMED Process (discussed in Part Two) so it's good to become familiar with them.

CHAPTER 1

WHY WE SUFFER AND HOW MINDFULNESS HELPS

My aim in writing this book is to introduce you to mindfulness methods that will help reduce your psychological suffering, enhance your fulfillment and expand and deepen your comfort, ease, contentment, peace, joy and happiness.

If you're a healing professional, these methods will almost certainly amplify the effectiveness of whatever therapeutic protocols you currently employ.

Before a physician can prescribe a cure, they need to clearly understand the primary cause of the illness. Likewise, for you to benefit most deeply from the mindfulness methods presented in this book, it's important to begin by learning a little about psychological suffering. How is it created? What are the dynamics that maintain it? Only then can you understand clearly how suffering can be resolved via the practice of mindfulness.

So, let's explore this issue of suffering. To begin, let's call suffering the "bother" or the "imposition" that the mind and body has on your sense of peacefulness and wellbeing. For example, most of us consider experiences of physical pain, grief, sadness, disappointment, loss and other negative emotions and sensations to be significant sources of bother or imposition. When we experience these things – and feel bothered by them – we say that we are suffering.

OUR HUMAN EXPERIENCE

Now let's look more closely at the fundamental aspects of our human experience and discuss how each is involved in this experience of suffering.

THE INTERNAL WORLD

As you know from your own experience, human beings have an **internal world** consisting of thoughts, mental images and feelings (emotional sensations). This internal world is mostly private: under normal circumstances, your thinking is not available to anyone else. In other words, other people can't know for sure what kind of self-talk, internal imagery and emotional sensations you are experiencing.

Notice that what we usually call "thinking" has two main components. One component of thinking is mental pictures of people, places, objects and situations. The other component of thinking is self-talk – our internal, verbal dialogue. What we refer to as emotional "feelings" are often a combination of physical sensations and thinking (internal talk and/or imagery).

In terms of emotional repair, we're especially interested in this aspect of human experience – thoughts, mental images and feelings – because it is within these realms that psychological suffering arises. Unwinding the various strands of this internal experience via mindfulness practice is a powerful tool for relieving suffering. (You'll learn a lot more about this via the Focus In instruction in Chapter 5.)

THE EXTERNAL WORLD

Of course, we also perceive the **external world** via our sense organs: our eyes, ears, nose, tongue and skin. We infer this external world to be shared with other living beings. Shifting attention from the internal world of self-talk, internal imagery and emotional sensations to the sights, sounds and tactile sensations of the external world is one way to use mindfulness to help unwind psychological suffering. (You'll learn a lot more about this via the Focus Out instruction in Chapter 5.)

OCCASIONAL AND ABSOLUTE REST

Our human experience also (and importantly!) includes occasional **periods of rest** – the *absence* of internal or external perceptual experience. For example, each time you close your eyes you experience the absence of external visual phenomena. And no matter how speedy your mental chatter may become, there are at least micro-moments of internal silence when there is the absence of thinking.

And, finally, there is the *awareness* that is the ever-present witness of these phenomena: the still point of absolute rest. Allowing sensory phenomena to be fully penetrated by, soaked in and transparent to – and hence most intimately *known by* – awareness is a vital component of mindfulness practice. (You'll learn a lot more about how accessing restful states can help you release psychological suffering and access profound realms of comfort and ease via the Focus on Rest instruction in Chapter 4.)

SUFFERING OR FREEDOM?

How we relate to these aspects of our human experience determines whether we experience psychological suffering or freedom. When we are identified with, caught up in, trapped in, swept away by, overwhelmed by or controlled by our thoughts, emotions or physical sensations, we experience psychological suffering. More on this in a moment.

But what about internal freedom? How is this best understood?

THE SPONTANEOUS FLOW OF THE NATURAL WORLD

We can begin to learn about internal freedom by observing the natural world. The branches of a tree sway in the wind; snow falls gently or blizzard-like in winter; flowers bloom every spring; earthquakes shake the ground; volcanoes lie dormant and then erupt; floods surge uncontrollably and then recede into stillness; stars appear at night and go into hiding during the day; and so on. Nature does what it does and there is no resistance coming from anywhere. There is a *just happening* quality about it. The cycles of the natural world ebb and flow, arise and dissolve, just as they are – in spontaneous alignment with (it would seem) a deep intelligence.

Our human body–minds are also parts of nature. But various levels of mental and emotional conditioning often prevent the natural, spontaneous flow of thinking, feeling and sensation. Physical or psychic contractions born of unexamined subconscious beliefs and habitual patterns of behaviour distort the flow of natural intelligence.

Consciously and subconsciously, we habitually feel *I want pleasure* and *I don't want pain*. However, if nature happens to be giving us physical or emotional pleasure, then that is the current reality of nature. The reality of nature is also that pleasure doesn't last.

And if nature happens to be giving us physical or emotional pain, then that is the current reality of nature. That reality provides us with important information. The reality of nature is also that this pain, whether chronic or acute, is naturally in a state of flux. Pain and pleasure alike are impermanent, ever-changing, ephemeral phenomena: experiences that come and go, moment by moment.

ALLOWING THE MIND–BODY TO DANCE AND FLOW

Mindfulness practice supports us in learning to relate to both pleasure and pain, both pleasant and unpleasant experience, just as they are – as natural phenomena – rather than as we hope, or wish, or demand them to be. We learn to relax and welcome sensory phenomena, giving them lots of space, rather than tensing up and turning away from them.

When we learn to relate to sensory phenomena in this way, we also learn to eliminate any internal friction – any resistance toward our current mind–body experience. Without resistance, the subjective experience of psychological suffering ceases.

Thoughts, emotions, sensations and perceptions can then dance and flow – just like the dance and flow of a river, a cloud or a blossoming (and then withering) flower – with a deeper dimension of *You* (the awareness that is aware of these words, right now) as their ever-present witness.

Living this way takes practice but anyone can do it. The simple techniques in this book will teach you how to flow with nature and will help you train away the response of fighting with your mind–body experience – of being "bothered" by it.

OUR YEARNING FOR HAPPINESS

Now, let's explore our desire for happiness and see how it can potentially get us into trouble.

It is completely natural for us to seek happiness, peace, joy, contentment, fulfillment, comfort and ease. The problem is that our recipes for happiness – which we inherited from our parents, teachers, culture and media – tend to be faulty. They simply don't (and can't possibly) deliver the happiness we yearn for because they are based upon faulty premises.

What are these faulty premises, which render our recipes for happiness more like recipes for misery? There are two primary culprits:

FAULTY PREMISE #1 – HOARDING AND AVOIDING

According to this faulty premise, the ticket to lasting happiness lies in aggressively running after and hoarding pleasurable sensations and stridently avoiding or eliminating painful sensations. Here is another way to say this: we divide all worldly phenomena into two categories – "good" and "bad" or "right" and "wrong" – and we believe that lasting happiness depends upon capturing (and forcefully detaining) the good/right and strongly rejecting the bad/wrong.

FAULTY PREMISE #2 – A PERMANENT, SEPARATE "ME"

According to this faulty premise, the presumed beneficiary of pleasant sensations and the presumed victim of painful sensations is a permanent, autonomous and independently existing "me" – rigidly separate from all "others." This mistaken assumption is sometimes referred to as a fixation on a separate self. Basically, it's a case of mistaken identity.

Now let's take a closer look at each of these faulty premises, see how mindfulness training can help us to release them and discover how we can align more intimately with genuine peace and happiness.

THE LOWDOWN ON PAIN AND PLEASURE

The **first faulty premise** has to do with our understanding of pleasure and pain. We're in the habit of trying to permanently eliminate pain and hold on to pleasure, instead of understanding that pleasant, unpleasant and neutral sensations are natural phenomena, which come and go, ebb and flow – just like all other natural phenomena. Let's take a closer look at this tendency and how it gets us into trouble.

At any given instance, we can classify our sensory experience as being either pleasant or unpleasant, or a mixture of pleasant and unpleasant, or as neutral (as neither pleasant nor unpleasant). If you'd like, you can experiment with this as you go through your day – pausing to notice if you'd call your current experience pleasant, unpleasant, a mix of the two or neutral.

We can refer to the pleasantness/pleasure or unpleasantness/ pain of a specific experience as its "affective valence" or its "hedonic valence." In this case, the word "hedonic" simply means "having to do with pleasure or pain." It's the degree of pleasure or pain – the subjective sense of pleasantness or unpleasantness – that we associate with a given sensory experience.

These pleasurable or painful sensations may be experienced primarily in the body – for example, the pleasure of receiving a warm hug from a friend or the pain of having a sprained ankle. Or, it might be experienced in the mind as a specific content or organization of thoughts (internal images and mental dialogue) that are either brilliantly and pleasurably uplifting or painfully confused.

Hedonic valence can be also experienced within the realm of emotional body sensations – the pleasantness of feeling joy, contentment, curiosity, hope, interest, pride, amusement, inspiration, awe, kindness and love; and the unpleasantness of feeling anger, anxiety, sadness, fear, shame, resentment, loneliness, guilt, frustration, despair, disappointment, jealousy and so on.

Our evaluation of an experience as pleasant, unpleasant or neutral can also occur in relation to the external environment – the sights, sounds, tastes, scents and tactile sensations that we encounter as we move through the world. A museum exhibit of William Blake sketches and paintings might be experienced by one person as pleasant, by another person as unpleasant and by a third person as a neutral *"meh."* And the same is true of a music concert or a culinary creation or a particular perfume. A forest trail or a high-mountain meadow on a sunny day may be experienced as quite pleasant, but on a windy, cold day as decidedly unpleasant.

So, once again: the hedonic valence – the evaluation of a sensory experience as pleasant, unpleasant, a mix of pleasant and unpleasant or as neutral – can occur in relation to physical, mental–emotional or external worldly experience. It can also occur within the realm of restful states – which many people experience as pleasant, but others as uncomfortable or mostly neutral.

THE NATURALNESS OF *LEANING TOWARD* PLEASANT EXPERIENCE

Now, it's quite natural to *lean toward* what we find to be pleasant and to *lean away* from what we experience as painful. These are natural human inclinations – a kind of inner GPS that helps keep the body–mind safe and properly oriented within its environment. In and of themselves, they are not a problem.

However, engaging in heavy-handed attraction/repulsion dynamics in a futile attempt to *permanently* acquire pleasant sensations and *permanently* avoid or eliminate unpleasant sensations creates all kinds of internal resistance. When we do this, we are at war with ourselves: strongly grasping at and attaching to some experiences (the pleasurable ones), and strongly repulsed by and pushing away other experiences (the painful ones).

As such, the spectrum of pleasant–neutral–unpleasant sensation is not a problem, and it doesn't *necessarily* have anything to do with suffering. What create psychological suffering are emotionally charged attraction/repulsion dynamics, which are rooted in our belief in an autonomous, permanent, independently existent self – that is the presumed beneficiary of the pleasant sensations and victim of unpleasant sensations.

SUFFERING, PURIFICATION, FRUSTRATION AND FULFILLMENT

The internal *friction* and *resistance* generated by such heavy-handed craving and repulsion is the immediate cause of psychological suffering. We can understand this more clearly by thinking about it this way, using the mathematical multiplication symbol:

Suffering = discomfort × resistance
Purification = discomfort × equanimity
Frustration = pleasure × resistance
Fulfillment = pleasure × equanimity

As you probably remember from your high-school math classes, any number multiplied by zero equals zero. So, for example: $10 \times 0 = 0$ and $50 \times 0 = 0$. The same principle applies in terms of the relationship between resistance and suffering: If our internal *resistance* to an uncomfortable or painful sensation is zero, then our level of psychological *suffering* will also be zero – regardless of how intense the pain might be.

When you grasp how truly profound and revolutionary this is, I can pretty much guarantee that you'll become a lifelong fan of equanimity!

EQUANIMITY AS SENSORY CONDUCTIVITY

Let's explore each of the four equations listed above in a bit more detail. To assist us, we'll be employing the notion of conductivity. In physics, chemistry and biology, *conductivity* is the measure of the ease with which either heat or an electric charge can pass through a material. So, in this context, a *conductor* is any material that gives very little resistance to the flow of thermal (heat) energy or an electric current. An example of electrical conductivity is how a home's wiring (made of copper, aluminum or another conductive material) carries electricity, which enables the ceiling lights and floor lamps to turn on when a switch is flipped.

And here's where mindfulness training comes in. We can think of equanimity (one of the three main components of mindfulness) as the *conductivity* of our sensory channels – their capacity to function without internal resistance. In other words, conductivity is a measure of how responsive a particular sensory network (for example, seeing, hearing or feeling) is to information and influence. A network that is working well is easily enriched by new information, and in terms of behaviour is motivated and directed by hedonic valence – an accurate understanding of what brings true and lasting happiness and genuine fulfillment.

Another way of saying that we experience sensory phenomena with equanimity or without resistance is to say that the sensory channel is fully *conductive*. So, once again, we can understand equanimity as a kind of sensory conductivity.

FULFILLMENT AND PURIFICATION: FLOWING WITH CONDUCTIVITY

Let's return now to the two equations from page 11 that feature equanimity:

Fulfillment = pleasure × equanimity
Purification = discomfort × equanimity

The degree to which a sensory channel is *conductive* – equanimity is functioning there – has an immediate effect on the hedonic valence (the evaluation of the pleasantness or unpleasantness) of the sensory experience.

Pleasant sensations experienced in a *conductive state* increase **fulfillment** and decrease craving and neediness. In the presence of equanimity – aka sensory conductivity – we don't become addicted to the pleasant sensations nor dependent upon them for our ultimate wellbeing. In the absence of internal resistance, pleasant sensations become even more pleasant and genuinely fulfilling.

Unpleasant sensations experienced in a *conductive state* – experienced with equanimity – create **less suffering** in terms of our subjective perception of the situation. They also tend to motivate and direct our behaviour in useful ways. In addition, uncomfortable or painful sensations can even elicit a kind of **joy of purification**. In such cases, the unpleasant sensation takes on a positive value, as a form of purification. This can be seen in certain ascetic practices such as fasting, sexual abstinence, sleep deprivation or secluding oneself in a forest hut or high-mountain cave. The hardship, discomfort and painful sensations are skillfully transformed via equanimity into the joy of purification.

But the joy of purification doesn't require extreme ascetic practice. Any unpleasant sensation that is embraced with equanimity can elicit a sense of something positive. Any moment of appreciation for how your application of equanimity has reduced or prevented psychological suffering may be accompanied by subtle (or more pronounced) pleasant sensations. This, also, is the joy of purification.

SUFFERING AND FRUSTRATION: NON-CONDUCTIVE RESISTANCE

The two equations from page 11 that feature internal resistance – a lack of equanimity – are:

Suffering = discomfort × resistance

Frustration = pleasure × resistance

When the sensory channels are not conductive – when there is little or no equanimity – then perceptions and behaviours are diminished by suffering and tend to be compulsive, driven and distorted. When sensory channels are non-conductive in this way, the flow of energy and information is stifled and inefficient, and the result is suffering and frustration.

Pleasant sensations experienced in a *non-conductive state* – without equanimity – tend to elicit neediness, craving and frustration – and hence become less pleasant over time.

Unpleasant sensations experienced in a *non-conductive state* – without equanimity – generate psychological suffering. This is an added layer of discomfort that's entirely unnecessary and compounds the original injury.

Once again: sensory conductivity – aka equanimity – makes pleasant sensations even more fulfilling, and "takes the edge off" of unpleasant sensations. For this reason, equanimity can play a central role in the improvement of a person's psychological wellbeing. It can help you vastly improve the quality of your life *even if you can't improve your circumstances.*

The even better news and a **key point** here is that equanimity is a **skill** that can be acquired and refined through mindfulness training – with methods like those shared in Chapters 4–8.

THE BOTTOM LINE: EQUANIMITY IS A REALLY GOOD THING

Equanimity offers a container within which to hold the full range of our human experience: the pleasant, the unpleasant and the neutral. The more that we can replace internal resistance with equanimity – a neutral, even-minded, nonreactive inner balance – the more we dissolve psychological suffering and amplify fulfillment and happiness. The mental imperturbability (along with physical relaxation) of equanimity protects us from emotional agitation and reactivity – and opens the way to lasting peace and happiness. (You'll be learning even more about equanimity in Chapter 2.)

HOW MINDFULNESS HELPS RELIEVE SUFFERING

Mindfulness methods can help us transform our relationship with pleasure and pain. They can help us experience painful sensations without the added (and unnecessary) psychological suffering caused by internally resisting them. And they can help us experience pleasurable sensations more fully – without expecting them to last forever. Experiencing pleasure without craving or neediness fosters genuine fulfillment, without the suffering that often comes when the pleasant experience inevitably comes to an end.

In other words, mindfulness supports a very different inner experience when it comes to difficult physical or emotional states. With mindfulness practice you can learn to experience grief, anxiety, anger, a headache or any other challenging emotional or physical circumstances with much less or even *no* sense of imposition or bother – without psychological suffering. Mindfulness supports this growing ability and willingness to experience things just as they are – to welcome the totality of your human experience without internal resistance.

Once again (it's worth repeating!): a human being can experience emotional and physical pain/discomfort with diminished or even a total absence of psychological suffering. This may sound strange at first, but it is absolutely true that you can experience yourself in this way with consistent mindfulness practice. You can have a taste of this kind of freedom, sometimes in your first practice session.

Mindfulness is a unique and powerful tool to help you resurrect your naturalness: the body–mind's inherent intelligence and the peace, joy and freedom at the core of your being. It teaches you how to fully welcome impermanence, and let nature take its course within your mind and body. Then feelings, thoughts and physical sensations flow naturally without turning into suffering. Even your sense of "self" can then be experienced as a flowing natural activity.

SEEING SELF AS AN ACTIVITY RATHER THAN AS A STATIC "THING"

The **second faulty premise** (from page 8) – which turns our natural desire for happiness into suffering – has to do with the presumed beneficiary of pleasant sensations and the presumed victim of painful sensations. We believe in a permanent, separate,

16

autonomous and independently existing "me" that experiences pleasure and pain. Whether we take this limited separate self to be a human body, a human mind, a human soul or a separate personal consciousness, the mistake is to assume that this entity is unchanging, permanent and inherently personal.

This is the root cause of our psychological suffering because it is on behalf of this (wholly imaginary) entity that we engage in the heavy-handed grasping and repulsion dynamics that create suffering.

Mindfulness practice helps us see clearly that both the human body (comprised of the elements of the natural world) and the human mind (the ostensible psychological self) are not static, permanent entities – but rather are ever-changing fluid *activities*.

Seeing this with utmost clarity allows us to release our various mistaken identities. This, in turn, helps us relax the habitual grasping/repulsion habits that generate internal friction, turbulence and resistance. Without this internal friction, the flow of sensory experience – our human experience – becomes effortlessly complete and infinitely fulfilling.

OVERCOMING CONFUSION: WHAT'S REALLY GOING ON HERE?

We began this chapter by invoking the metaphor of a doctor diagnosing a disease and then prescribing appropriate medicine. Similarly, we can apply the medicine of mindfulness to extricate ourselves from unnecessary suffering and reestablish the internal freedom that is our natural state.

Mindfulness training – either on its own or in conjunction with more conventional therapeutic modalities – offers a powerful antidote to psychological suffering. What makes mindfulness such a powerful medicine is how it can help us see more clearly what's really going on in our experience. In other words, it helps us overcome confusion.

So far, we've discussed two primary causes of psychological suffering: 1) heavy-handed attachment/repulsion dynamics, and 2) the mistaken belief in a permanent, unchanging, autonomous, separate self. For each of these, mindfulness practice provides a remedy.

There is a third cause of psychological suffering: confusion. We ignore – or refuse to see clearly – what is actually happening. This kind of confusion, bewilderment or obfuscation can easily undermine our mental health.

CONFUSION AND MENTAL HEALTH

How does confusion around what's really happening contribute to mental–emotional disharmony? And how does mindfulness help us overcome this ignorance-rooted confusion and restore mental health? Let's consider a couple of examples.

If you're feeling emotionally overwhelmed, you may be consciously aware only that you are freaking out – and everything else is eclipsed by this. Or, if you're experiencing a compulsion to do something harmful, you may only be aware of the most surface-level urge: *I simply **must** do this, right now!* In other words, your perception of what's happening is entirely superficial. Thoughts, sensations and emotions are tangled up into a dense mass of charged experience and impulses – preventing any kind of nuanced perception or genuine clarity in relation to your circumstances.

When we suffer, we often experience our thoughts and feelings as tangled up in this way. However, with the support of mindfulness techniques, you'll learn to untangle the strands of sensory experience – thoughts, images, feelings and perceptions – by noting and labeling them. (You'll learn all about this in Chapter 3.) This process enhances clarity and opens the door to authentic understanding. It supports a release of unnecessary suffering and the restoration of psychological harmony.

THE MEDICINE OF MICROSCOPIC WELCOMING AWARENESS

Mindfulness helps you become more clearly aware of what is going on in any given moment within the mind–body process. You are bringing nonjudgmental awareness, at a microscopic level, to what is arising within you. This kind of mindful awareness is the medicine that cures the suffering (the sense of bother or imposition) around the issue because it allows thoughts and feelings to flow freely – to pass right through – rather than getting stuck and feeling as solid as frozen icebergs.

When psychological suffering is relieved through mindfulness training, then we don't have to relieve it (temporarily) by engaging in destructive behaviours such as compulsive eating, drinking, doing drugs, having unsafe sex, spending hours scrolling social media feeds, overworking, etc. We've discovered another recipe for happiness – namely, mindfulness training – that actually works.

Ultimately, mindfulness is about unconditional freedom. Why? Because we discover that we don't *need* to change any circumstance – within the body, mind or world – to experience an infinite inner reservoir of peacefulness and joy. This profound insight releases us from the bondage of being compulsively driven to hold onto worldly pleasure and push away pain/discomfort. Instead, we can allow the body and mind to flow naturally, with comfort and ease.

REVEALING WHAT'S OPERATING BEHIND THE SCENES

As you begin using the Unified Mindfulness techniques introduced in Chapters 4–8, you'll cultivate the capacity to see more clearly what previously had been hidden from you, operating behind the scenes subconsciously. You'll perceive with clarity what's *really* going on when you suffer. You'll accurately understand the dynamics of psychological suffering. And this is the first step on the road to emotional repair – to resolving psychological disturbances and nourishing your mental health and wellbeing.

With the support of mindfulness methods, you'll learn to directly observe, in subtle detail, how self and world are created and dissolved moment by moment. Through this direct perception you'll be able to untangle the previously enmeshed strands of sensory experience. This will open possibilities for untangling or dissolving psychological suffering completely. You'll discover freedom from urges and impulses that you previously felt compelled to act upon. And you'll become newly aware of inner resources that can nourish ever-expanding levels of wellbeing.

DIAGNOSING THE DISEASE

Imagine you have a disease that no one has yet been able to diagnose. Your healing can't begin yet and the appropriate medicine cannot yet be prescribed. Similarly, it's only after you've completed a thorough investigation of your thoughts, feelings and physical sensations – and added the elixir of equanimity – that you can discover a cure for the disease of psychological suffering.

When you are largely unconscious of your mind–body processes, this lack of awareness sets the stage for destructive attitudes, beliefs and behaviours – which can escalate into bona fide mental illnesses. It's important to get in touch with these processes. Mindful awareness is a tool for doing just this, and it can help release their control over you.

The mindfulness methods provided in this book will help you develop this more nuanced awareness and understanding of your body–mind. With practice, mindfulness will become natural and spontaneous, helping you live a life of ever-increasing inner peace and joy.

Now, let's take an even closer look at mindfulness itself. What exactly is mindfulness and how does it help relieve psychological suffering?

WHAT IS MINDFULNESS?

Chances are good that you've already come across the word *mindfulness*. It's used a lot these days in a variety of ways. For our purposes here, we're going to begin with a very intuitive meaning of the word, which is simply *to keep something in mind* or *to remember something*. When we are mindfully aware of something, we keep it in mind, moment by moment. For example, to be mindful of your breath is to keep the breath *in mind*: to remember to pay attention to your breathing (how it sounds and how it feels in the body) in a gently focused way, again and again. You allow your attention to be fully absorbed by the breath.

This ability to attend to things we deem important or relevant – and to remain gently focused on them – requires us to be alert, watchful and committed to doing our best.

The opposite of mindfulness is distraction: having your attention pulled away from what you've decided to attend to.

An important part of mindfulness is the ability to remind yourself, moment by moment, to *return* to paying attention to, say, the breath, especially if your mind has wandered or you've begun to daydream. If I'm watching my breath – following its inhalations and exhalations – and then drift off into thinking about what I'm going to have for lunch, this is a distraction. At some point, I notice that I'm thinking about lunch. Then I bring myself back to attending to – being mindful of – the breath. The moment I notice distraction, mindfulness reappears.

As you become more and more familiar with mindfulness practice – and as you systematically train your attention skills – your capacity to maintain attentive continuity with any chosen object will increase. Little by little, the moments of mindfulness will become more and more of an uninterrupted stream of mindfulness. And as you'll see, this streaming, flowing mindfulness is deeply healing – and deeply enjoyable.

HOW MINDFULNESS WORKS

Do you ever notice that certain thoughts and feelings have a sticky, gummy, gluey quality – they adhere and cling to you in an annoying way and you can't quite free yourself of them? Mindfulness helps to dissolve the glue. It teaches us how to get out of the way of our thoughts, feelings and sensations – to give them lots of space – so that they can arise, transform and dissolve in their naturally impermanent way. So, let's explore a bit more deeply how exactly this happens.

As you become familiar with mindfulness practices, you will begin to see more clearly how the "story of myself" – the idea of who you are – is created. You'll see how this "me-story" or "self-story" is an interweaving of thoughts, internal images and feelings that are either reproduced or transformed, moment by moment.

Likewise, you will come to understand more clearly how the "story of the world" – your perceptions and ideas about the external world – also are created, moment by moment. You'll also begin to see how the "self-story" and the "world-story" deeply influence and interpenetrate one another.

THE THEATRE OF "SELF" AND "WORLD"

As you more clearly perceive these strands of sensory experience – the thoughts, feelings, images and perceptions that constitute "self" and "world" – you'll recognize their ever-changing and impermanent nature, as well as your capacity to both witness and transform them.

You can then appreciate the "self-story" and the "world-story" as you might appreciate a good movie, a novel or a theatrical play – from the point of view of the audience witnessing the production, as well as from a behind-the-scenes point of view, understanding a bit about how it's all being created.

With the support of mindfulness practice, you will learn to *appreciate* "self" and "world" in the way that a viewer appreciates a film. You can *transcend* "self" and "world" in the sense of no longer feeling stuck in, or oppressed by, your "self-story" and "world-story." This is akin to how someone watching a movie doesn't feel threatened by whatever is happening in it. And, to an extent, you can also *improve* "self" and "world," in the same way that the writer and director of a film can influence its setting, its events, and the behaviour of its characters.

TWO WAYS OF LOOKING AT MINDFULNESS PRACTICE

There are two ways to look at the practice of mindfulness – and both are valid:

1. Mindfulness is an exercise, something that we do to achieve a result. Mindfulness techniques *create* concentration, clarity and equanimity.
2. Mindfulness is natural. Mindfulness techniques simply *allow* concentration, clarity and equanimity to happen – they *unveil* what is already (and has always been) here.

In the first way of understanding mindfulness, it's something that is developed or cultivated. In the second way, it's your natural state waiting to be fully recognized.

Here is how Shinzen Young articulates this dual nature of mindfulness practice:

"On one hand, practice involves cultivated improvement. On the other hand, it involves noticing a primordial perfection that's always there. The fact that there are these two sides to practice has historically led to much confusion in both East and West. But the resolution is clear. Just as physicists eventually had to resign themselves to the fact that light has a dual nature (spreading wave, particulate chunk), just so contemplatives must resign themselves to the fact that practice has a dual nature. It can involve a mandate to make intentional improvements, but it also can involve a mandate to see that there's nothing to be improved."

As you continue reading this book, you will have the opportunity to apply its mindfulness techniques to specific instances of psychological suffering. This will set the stage for deep, radical and positive transformation.

SUMMARY

- Mindfulness is keeping something gently and clearly in mind, and coming back to it each time you get distracted. The moment you notice distraction, mindfulness returns.
- Mindfulness is cultivated through having one or more specific practices, such as the ones described in this book.
- Mindfulness helps relieve psychological suffering by making us deeply aware of the ever-changing impermanent nature of the "self-story" and the "world-story" – so we're less likely to succumb to push-and-pull dynamics with our body–mind experience.
- There are two ways of looking at mindfulness practice: 1) as an exercise that *creates* concentration, clarity and equanimity; and 2) as a process that *unveils* the concentration, clarity and equanimity that are always and already naturally present. Both are valid and, in concert, can be mutually enhancing.

CHAPTER 2

WHAT IS UNIFIED MINDFULNESS?

Unified Mindfulness is a specific type of mindfulness training developed by mindfulness teacher and neuroscience consultant Shinzen Young. It includes a multitude of different techniques – six of which are introduced in this book.

Unified Mindfulness is also the type of mindfulness training upon which my Unified Mindfulness Exposure and Desensitization (UMED) Process – the primary focus of this book – is based. To become adept at applying the UMED Process, you'll first learn (in Chapters 4–8) several Unified Mindfulness techniques.

The basic components of mindfulness that Shinzen highlights in his Unified Mindfulness system are *concentration, clarity* and *equanimity*.

1. **Concentration** is the ability to focus on what you deem relevant. It's the capacity to rest attention on a chosen field of inquiry and hold it there for as long as you wish to – coming back whenever you notice that you've been distracted. Developing concentration is a key component to freedom from suffering. It helps you develop the mental clarity that is necessary to unwind entangled mental–emotional strands of experience, which is key to releasing psychological suffering.

All of the Unified Mindfulness methods that you learn in this book will involve concentration, which is also a wonderful asset when it comes to fully experiencing and appreciating the pleasures of life.

2. **Clarity** is the ability to detect and untangle the strands of your experience. A key aspect of clarity involves noticing how sensory phenomena can be fully penetrated by, soaked with, and opened to awareness. Sensory experience and its background of awareness are noticed simultaneously. You see clearly that your experience of sensory phenomena always arises within the field of awareness and is inseparable from it.

3. **Equanimity** is an inner balance that represents a middle way: a third possibility between the extremes of suppressing (pushing away) and grasping (reaching for) sensory experiences. Equanimity is the capacity for neutral, nonreactive observation of sensory experience – for "keeping your cool" and remaining poised, even in the face of challenging circumstances. It enables us to maintain mental and emotional evenness rather than be drawn into charged attraction or repulsion dynamics.

   A key aspect of equanimity is the ability not to fight or interfere with ourselves at any level. Also, with equanimity, discomfort (painful sensations) causes less suffering and pleasure (pleasant sensations) provides more fulfillment.

Each of the Unified Mindfulness techniques you'll read about enhances concentration, clarity and equanimity. Collectively, they have the power to enhance the quality of your experience across the board, and to support freedom from suffering and the flowering of deep insight.

Now, let's take a closer look at the third component of mindfulness: equanimity. Because of its potent capacity to unwind psychological suffering – as well as to enhance fulfillment – Shinzen Young often refers to equanimity as an elixir.

In the section below Shinzen provides additional details, as he sings the praises of this most-valuable psychological resource.

THE ELIXIR OF EQUANIMITY

Equanimity is a fundamental skill for self-exploration and emotional intelligence. It is a deep and subtle concept frequently misunderstood and easily confused with suppression of feeling, apathy, indifference or inexpressiveness.

Equanimity comes from the Latin word *aequus*, meaning balanced, and *animus*, meaning spirit or internal state. As an initial step in understanding this concept, let's consider for a moment its opposite: what happens when a person loses internal balance.

In the physical world we say a person has lost balance if they fall to one side or another. In the same way, a person loses internal balance if they fall into one or the other of the following contrasting reactions:

1. **Suppression** – when an internal or external sensory experience arises and we attempt to cope with it by rejecting or denying it, stuffing it down, tightening around it and so on.
2. **Identification** – when an internal or external sensory experience arises and we fixate on it, hold onto it inappropriately and don't let it arise, spread and pass with its natural rhythm.

Between suppression on one side and identification on the other lies a third possibility: the balanced state of non-self-interference, or equanimity – in body and mind.

- **Equanimity in Body** is maintaining a continuous relaxed state over your whole body as sensations (pleasant, unpleasant, strong, subtle, physical, emotional) wash through.
- **Equanimity in Mind** is letting go of negative judgments about what you are experiencing or replacing them with an attitude of loving acceptance and gentle matter-of-factness.

EQUANIMITY AND MENTAL HEALTH: HAVING YOUR CAKE AND EATING IT TOO

Equanimity belies the adage that you cannot "have your cake and eat it too." When you apply equanimity to unpleasant sensations, they flow more readily and as a result cause less suffering. When you apply equanimity to pleasant sensations, they also flow more readily and as a result deliver deeper fulfillment. So, the same skill positively affects both ends of the sensation spectrum.

Furthermore, when feelings are experienced with equanimity, they cease to drive and distort behaviour and instead assume their proper function of skillfully motivating and directing it. Thus, equanimity plays a critical role in changing negative behaviours such as substance and alcohol abuse, compulsive eating, anger, violence and so on.

You can also have equanimity with thoughts. You can let positive and negative thoughts come and go without push or pull. You can let sense and nonsense (rational and irrational thoughts) arise and pass without preferring one over the other. This will result in a new kind of knowing – a kind of wisdom function, known within the Eastern contemplative traditions as *prajna*: transcendental wisdom, intuitive insight and an understanding of the true nature of phenomena.

Equanimity with thoughts also allows you to work through the compulsive drive to think. When compulsive eaters work through the drive to eat, they don't stop eating, they simply eat in a new and better way. As such, when compulsive thinkers (just about everyone) work through the drive to think, they don't stop thinking, they just begin to think in a new and better way.

EQUANIMITY, APATHY AND SUPPRESSION

Equanimity is sometimes confused with apathy, but they are completely different. Equanimity involves non-interference with the natural flow of sensory experience. Apathy implies indifference to the controllable outcome of objective events. So, although equanimity and apathy seem similar, they are actually opposites. Equanimity frees up internal energy for responding to external situations.

By definition, equanimity involves a radical permission to experience your senses – and, as such, is the opposite of suppression. As far as external expression of feeling is concerned, internal equanimity gives one the freedom to externally express or not, depending on what is appropriate to the situation.

A WORD ABOUT INTERNAL vs EXTERNAL PASSIVITY

It's important to realize that becoming internally passive, receptive and spacious via the mindfulness practice of equanimity does *not* imply that you will become *externally* passive. In fact, becoming internally passive will actually allow you to become *more* active and efficient in your activities out in the world. By eliminating the habitual and subtle fighting with thoughts and feelings, you free up energy that previously dissipated through internal friction. This freeing up of energy also enhances creative expression.

Equanimity is to the mind–body what oil is to an automobile engine. In both cases, better lubrication leads to more efficient functioning.

* * *

After that detailed exploration of equanimity, which deeply supports the other two components of mindfulness: concentration and clarity, let's now shift gears a little and explore the overall benefits of a Unified Mindfulness practice.

THE BENEFITS OF UNIFIED MINDFULNESS TRAINING

As you'll soon experience for yourself, each specific Unified Mindfulness technique delivers its own set of benefits. But we can say that the most *general purpose* of Unified Mindfulness practice is to decrease suffering and elevate fulfillment. As Shinzen Young puts it:

> "Most people suffer when they experience emotional and physical pain. Mindfulness leads to an ability to have these unpleasant experiences with diminished or no anguish, and a greater ability to cope. It also leads to increased fulfillment with both pleasant and neutral life experiences."

The benefits of a consistent Unified Mindfulness practice can be quite wide-ranging and profound. They include:

- Relief – minimizing suffering
- Satisfaction – maximizing fulfillment
- Insight – understanding yourself at all levels
- Mastery – acting skillfully
- Service – serving from love

Depending on which specific techniques you employ, your Unified Mindfulness practice will allow you more to fully:

1. Appreciate "self" and "world": experience the senses with radical fullness.
2. Transcend "self" and "world": contact something beyond the senses.
3. Express spontaneity: develop energy and creativity in what you do, say and think.
4. Nurture the positive: selectively attend to positive emotions, rational thought and positive behaviours.
5. Refine your personhood.
6. Be of service to others.

Sounds pretty good, right? And it is! But how, exactly, does all this happen?

It happens by learning the Unified Mindfulness techniques and then being willing (and, I hope, excited) to practise them regularly. These techniques can be done daily as formal sitting meditation. They can also be employed more informally as you go about your daily activities.

In addition, it can be very beneficial to periodically practise mindfulness methods in a more intensive retreat setting: for an entire day, weekend or week.

Finally, it may be helpful – every now and again – to get support from an experienced Unified Mindfulness coach (see Resources). However, the instruction offered here in this book will get you started and provide a solid foundation for your mindfulness training.

MINDFULNESS AND MENTAL HEALTH: SHINZEN'S PERSPECTIVE

How are mindfulness training and conventional forms of psychotherapy and psychiatry similar, and how are they different? This is a question that I'm often asked and have addressed at some length in this book's introduction. Here are some additional thoughts and insights, along with a fascinating case study, that are related to this question – from Shinzen Young, the creator of the Unified Mindfulness system. The following sections are compiled from interviews conducted with Shinzen in 2017 and 2018.

So, in Shinzen's own words …

HOW THERAPY AND MINDFULNESS ARE SIMILAR

How are therapy and mindfulness similar? To begin, if we look at the terms that are used in therapy, many of them sound like aspects of mindfulness. For example, most therapists are going to encourage their clients to be more *aware of* what's going on. And they're going to say that when the person is not aware of what's going on, they are likely to feel less happy and will tend to take less-appropriate actions. Often, this encouragement to be more aware is expressed in questions such as, *"How does that make you feel?"*

But in such cases, the word *feel* is being used very vaguely. The therapist is probably asking the client not just what kind of body emotion they are experiencing, but also what kind of mental talk and mental images they're going through at that moment. So, there's an emphasis on the importance of reducing the effect of "unconsciousness" – the lack of present-moment awareness.

There also tends to be a lot of talk, within therapy sessions, about *reducing self-conflict* – about not fighting with yourself, and so on. There's talk about *being in the present moment* rather than inappropriately holding onto the past. There's talk about breaking up coagulations or knots in the depth of the client's being.

All of these actually sound very much like aspects of mindfulness practice. So, because there's a similarity in the words – in the terms that are employed – we have to ask: is one just another version of the other, or not? If we just look at the buzzwords, they seem to be talking about the same thing.

So, if I had to distinguish or disambiguate, I would say that many of the general things that a therapist will encourage do sound like the things that a mindfulness teacher will encourage. However, there are also some really important differences.

THERAPY VS MINDFULNESS: THE DOSING DIFFERENCE

First, there's a dosing difference, so to speak. A therapist is probably going to ask their client, every now and again, to be aware of something in the subconscious that is influencing them, or to be aware of what they're experiencing in this moment. The client may be asked to do this *every now and again*. But formal mindfulness training has a person doing this *constantly, incessantly* – hour after hour after hour. So, mindfulness training provides a much larger "dosage" of close attention to mind activity and sensory experience.

Also, a therapist may ask their client to learn how to be less conflicted, how to fight with themselves less often. But, once again, this instruction tends to be restricted to *occasionally* and with regard to a *specific issue*. In mindfulness training, a person is also learning how not to fight with themselves, but it's *ongoing and continuous*. It's at a millisecond level all day, so that eventually their senses go through a phase change and become fluid, as a result of this kind of ongoing application of non-self-interference.

I would say that, in mindfulness, we seriously expect a person to do things similar to what is done in therapy – but ten or a hundred or a thousand or ten-thousand times as intensely. And that's going make a big difference in terms of results.

So that's one difference between therapy and mindfulness: dosing. And if a particular form of therapy delivers the kind of intense dosing that I'm talking about here, then – by my definition – it has become mindfulness training.

THERAPY VS MINDFULNESS: THE SCOPE OF APPLICATION DIFFERENCE

The second difference between therapy and mindfulness training is that therapy tends to be much narrower in its application. This can actually be okay, because that gives it some specialness that may be needed by a mindfulness practitioner just as much as by any other client. I, myself, once needed 18 months of behaviourally oriented weekly sessions with a psychiatrist to help me make a behaviour change. This psychiatrist specialized in that area, and I needed that.

So, the fact that therapy might be *more specialized* isn't necessarily a negative. But it's important to realize that the relief from suffering that a person derives from successful mindfulness practice is *far broader* than what a person typically receives from successful therapy. For example, a successful mindfulness practitioner – a real pro – can experience fainting levels of physical pain with amazingly little perception of suffering, and intense levels of physical pleasure without even a hint of dualistic craving or attachment.

And I know of no forms of therapy that deliver this kind of thing. So, it's not just a matter of transforming a certain subset of thoughts. With a consistent mindfulness practice, the whole mind–body is set free at an industrial-strength level.

THERAPY VS MINDFULNESS: PATHOLOGY AND FULFILLMENT DIFFERENCES

Another difference between mindfulness practice and therapy is that therapy originally arose within the context of treating suffering or reducing perceived suffering that was at clearly pathological levels. For example, various therapies were developed to treat actual mental illnesses – conditions that receive a psychiatric diagnosis – which mindfulness training on its own may not be able to treat.

Also, though the reduction of suffering is certainly a goal of mindfulness training, elevation of overall wellbeing and fulfillment is also an important goal of mindfulness. And this points, once again, to how the goals of mindfulness are very broad.

MINDFULNESS, MENTAL ILLNESS AND *DUKKHA*

Now, this begs the question: are there mental illnesses that basically have nothing to do with the core sense of lack or dissatisfaction understood to be the root cause of suffering within contemplative traditions such as Buddhism and Hinduism? Or in more technical terms, are there mental illnesses that have nothing to do with *dukkha* – which is the Pali and Sanskrit term (Sanskrit: दुःख; Pali: *dukkha*) often translated into English as suffering, pain or unhappiness. It means something that is uneasy, unsteady, uncomfortable, unpleasant or dissatisfactory. It refers to the prevalent sense of lack – of not being at ease – when driven by craving/grasping, repulsion/aversion and ignorance.

And my answer to this question would be that there are certain mental illnesses that – as one aspect of their treatment – might involve mindfulness techniques. (Examples of this can be found in Part Two of this book, which describe Shelly's application of the UMED Process.) However, there are also severe psychological imbalances that are genuine medical conditions, and they require medical/psychiatric intervention.

The bottom line is that mindfulness training is not a medical intervention. It can be an adjunct, a helper to a medical intervention, but if a person has bipolar disorder, severe clinical depression or schizophrenia, they may well need some medication and will definitely need to see a mental health professional for that.

WHY MINDFULNESS WON'T ENTIRELY REPLACE THERAPY

Mindfulness can't claim to cure physiological conditions. Sometimes it might be helpful and part of the cure. And that's why mindfulness training will not entirely replace various forms of counseling, psychotherapy and psychiatry. Mindfulness teachers, as such, are not trained to deal with specific mental illnesses. However, Shelly Young is a mindfulness teacher who *is* also trained to deal with mental illnesses. She can either handle them herself or refer someone to a psychiatrist when she knows that is more appropriate.

But mindfulness teachers in general don't have formal psychiatric training. I don't have that training, so I would never presume to be able to diagnose and treat someone along those lines.

That said, over the years and decades, I have worked with many, many people and while interacting with them I can usually get a sense of whether or not there might be a serious mental illness at play. While I would never officially diagnose someone, I might suggest that they see a medical professional. And I've trained all of my Unified Mindfulness coaches to do the same.

ASPECTS OF THERAPY THAT MINDFULNESS CAN REPLACE

Even though mindfulness training will never entirely replace therapy, my sense is that a lot of the things people go to therapists for are really just issues of general happiness; they're not actually psychiatric issues.

I suspect that a large percentage of people who go to a therapist are just seeking to elevate their happiness; to have less suffering and more fulfillment in their lives; to understand themselves at all levels; to change their behaviour; and to perhaps explore ways of being of greater service to their communities.

And if I were to make a prediction, my sense is that in the coming decades people who are now seeking therapy for these reasons will instead engage in mindfulness training. People will go to mindfulness professionals, and mindfulness training may to some degree replace therapy in cases where the primary issue is the baseline level of happiness and contentment.

So those are some of the similarities and differences between mindfulness training and psychotherapy, as I see it. There's a place for them both, which is a good thing, because each of them plays an important role.

A CASE STUDY FROM SHINZEN: MINDFULNESS AND THERAPY WORKING TOGETHER

When I encounter students who have serious psychological issues, I refer them to mental health professionals. That said, I have on several occasions worked in conjunction with psychiatrists. One example is working with a student who had a borderline personality disorder diagnosis and had been under the care of a psychiatrist.

This student was very devoted to mindfulness practice and asked me if I could help her with her borderline personality disorder. So, of course, the first thing I had to do was make sure that a mental health professional was involved in all this – because I wasn't going to try to do therapy. She assured me that she was seeing a psychiatrist, and I made sure that the psychiatrist thought it was okay for me to become involved in trying to help her with her borderline personality disorder. And the psychiatrist signed off on this, saying that it was fine to proceed.

So, as a first step, I asked this woman to describe to me her main symptoms. And she said, "Well, when I'm in the presence of another person, I lose my own identity. I don't know who I am anymore. The looming presence of 'other' just swamps me and I can't be myself. And this leads to a whole range of problems in my life ..." She then outlined those problems. But I got the picture; I saw what her basic problem was and did an analysis of it based upon the way I like to classify sensory experience.

Within meditation and mindfulness communities, one often hears statements such as – "You have to have a self before you can let go of a self." And some people even say that a person shouldn't meditate until they've "gotten themselves together" emotionally, psychologically. Why? Because meditation, in its essence, involves the deconstruction of the (egoic) small-self, and (according to this argument) you need to have a healthy strong self before you can meditate. Because if you try to deconstruct this egoic self and it hasn't been properly constructed, it can lead to problems.

However, I think that this kind of analysis is rather ham-fisted, clumsy. It lacks some subtlety, because there are many different meditation or mindfulness techniques – and even a single given technique can be used in a whole variety of ways.

In the case of this woman, she told me that her problem was losing contact with who she was whenever she was in the presence of an "other." Now, I have a technique I sometimes give people to deconstruct or untangle the small-self that, with a slight modification, can also be used to help a person more fully establish contact with their individual self in a clear and concentrated way.

So, I had her apply the Unified Mindfulness Focus In technique, which was to note and label her mental images as *see*, her mental talk as *hear* and her emotional body sensations as *feel* – and to speak these labels out loud. One way a person can use this technique is for the purpose of untangling those threads of experience, which eventually will reveal to them that there is no separate-self. But another way to use this very same Focus In technique is for anchoring a person more firmly in the activity of their own personality – which is their visual thought, their auditory thought and the emotions felt in their body.

So, with a slight modification of the technique, I supported this student in learning how to remain clearly concentrated on her inner state – her own unique personality – even as she exposed herself to progressively more impactful "others." And within a few years, she reported that she was essentially cured of this problem.

This case illustrates the powerful intersection of the two worlds of psychiatry and mindfulness training – and how they can be used together effectively.

* * *

I hope you enjoyed reading Shinzen's perspective on the relationship between mindfulness and mental health, and how a

Unified Mindfulness technique can be used in conjunction with psychiatric care. Quite inspiring, indeed!

MINDFULNESS AS AN UNBIASED AND SECULAR PATH

One of the strengths of Unified Mindfulness is that its power to dissolve psychological suffering and to reveal unconditioned freedom stands wholly independent from any social, political or religious organization and doesn't require any prior beliefs. While mindfulness practice may be – and historically has been – part of a formal spiritual path, it can also stand on its own. As Shinzen puts it:

> "What is revolutionary about mindfulness is that it makes the acquisition and application of attentional skills the centrepiece for potentially radical psycho-spiritual growth. It can therefore sidestep some of the contentious issues surrounding historical movements, where the centrepiece is often acceptance of a belief structure, combined with assent to a detailed list of rules."

Now that you've learned a bit about the potential benefits of mindfulness – and the Unified Mindfulness system in particular – you're ready to dive into the practice itself, which begins in the next chapter.

SUMMARY

- Unified Mindfulness is a user-friendly, science-informed system of mindfulness practice developed by Shinzen Young.
- The basic components highlighted and cultivated through Unified Mindfulness training are concentration, clarity and equanimity.
- The elixir of equanimity allows you to "have your cake and eat it too."
- Unified Mindfulness training reduces suffering, helps you understand yourself at all levels, helps you change behaviours, and fosters a spirit of service.
- There are both similarities and differences between mindfulness training and therapy – and each has an important role to play.
- Mindfulness practice is an integral aspect of several spiritual traditions. It can also be used independently of any religious or spiritual path, as is the case with Unified Mindfulness.

CHAPTER 3

HOW TO NOTE AND LABEL

In the same way that a raft and an oar are useful tools for navigating a lake, **noting** and **labeling** are useful tools for navigating mindfulness.

Eventually, you'll be able to swim in mindfulness, at which point the formal practices of noting and labeling become optional. But for now, it will be worth your while to become familiar with these tools.

WHAT IS NOTING?

To **note** a sensory experience means to *notice it* – to clearly acknowledge its appearance – and then to gently, intently *focus on it* for a few seconds (or until it vanishes).

So, for example, to *note* a flower you are looking at means to notice the seeing-of-the-flower clearly and then pause long enough to gently focus your gaze and attention upon it.

WHAT IS LABELING?

Labels are spoken words or thoughts that name the specific sensory experience you are focusing on. To **label** an internal or external sensory experience means to *think or say a word or phrase* that describes what you are noting.

If (as in the flower example) you are noting the seeing-of-a-flower, you might support this noting by applying the label *see*. You would then repeat – either out loud or internally, as a thought – the word *see* every few seconds, as a way to anchor your noting of the seeing-of-the-flower.

While it is possible to note without labeling, the labeling process can provide very useful support, particularly for beginners.

The things we note – and label – are aspects of our sensory experience: thoughts, internal images, feelings, sights, sounds, smells, tastes, tactile sensations and restful states. We can also note the moments in which any or all of these phenomena vanish or dissolve. Each of the Unified Mindfulness techniques that you will be learning in Chapters 4–8 will involve noting and labeling a specific subset of your sensory experience.

NOTING AND LABELING EXAMPLE

To take an example, you may note the sensation of your feet touching the floor by clearly *noticing* this sensation and gently *focusing* on it for a few seconds. (If you like, you can do this right now.)

As you note the sensation of your feet touching the floor, you may also *label* the sensation with the word *feel* (spoken aloud or internally as a thought), repeated in a gentle matter-of-fact voice, every few seconds.

Before applying the label *feel*, the sensation is just a sensation. The label *feel* clarifies the particular sensation you are attending to and supports the noting process.

MINDFULNESS, NOTING AND LABELING

What is the relationship between mindfulness, noting and labeling?

Noting is designed to facilitate mindfulness by anchoring your attention more fully into an appreciation of the here-and-now, with its everchanging phenomena. It helps to enhance concentration, clarity and equanimity – the fundamental components of mindfulness.

And **labeling** is designed to facilitate noting, by assigning a word or short phrase – a simple label – to the sensory experience that you are noting. This helps to clarify the experience you are noting. Labeling also gives your conceptual, thinking mind a specific job to do. This decreases the probability of it wandering off into thoughts or theories, or the past or the future.

WOUNDED WARRIOR:
HOW LABELING CAN SUPPORT
PSYCHOLOGICAL HEALING

The labeling process can be extremely useful in helping to unwind challenging mental–emotional patterns and supporting mental health and wellness. You'll see how this works for specific psychological conditions in Part Two of this book. To give you a preview ...

When you label in this way as part of your mindfulness practice, you're giving a simple basic name to your internal and/or external sensory experience, moment by moment. And this helps take the judgments and preconceptions out of the experience, so you don't have to suffer through it.

Instead, you see that the unpleasant experience – however intense it may seem – is no more than a changing, passing phenomenon. It's not who you are essentially. The labels help you realize that unpleasant emotional or physical conditions are not "you" – they don't define your true identity – but rather are ever-transforming and ephemeral natural processes that *You* (as the witnessing awareness) can mindfully observe.

A story that's often told to illustrate this is of a warrior who has just been shot by an arrow. In such a case, the wise thing for the warrior to do is to carefully remove the arrow, wash the wound and apply a healing poultice.

Noting and labeling the various thoughts, emotional feelings and physical sensations associated with an emotionally challenging experience is the equivalent of removing the arrow, washing the wound and applying a healing poultice.

Now, would it be wise for that warrior to take one of his own arrows out of his quiver and forcefully stab it into his fresh wound – creating a second wound within the first wound? Obviously, not!

Judgment, negative commentary and internal resistance – the body and mind contracting and spinning off into thoughts of the past and future – are like the second arrow plunged into the original wound. It just exacerbates the problem. It adds a layer of unnecessary psychological suffering to the challenging circumstances.

So, learning to note and label can help you avoid stabbing yourself with the second arrow. Instead, you apply the healing balm of mindfully noting and labeling – which kindly and intelligently supports the healing process.

NOTING AND LABELING
IN MORE DETAIL

Though the basics of noting and labeling are quite simple, there's an art and science to these practices that you can develop over time – and learn to apply with increasing levels of precision and subtlety.

The rest of this chapter offers more detailed guidance for skillfully cultivating these important tools, via questions posed directly to Shinzen Young – the founder of the Unified Mindfulness system – and his answers to these questions. Here, you'll likely find assistance for whatever roadblock you may encounter, in relation to noting and labeling. If you prefer, however, you can skip ahead to Chapter 4, and return to this more detailed exploration later.

THE TWO PARTS OF ANY ACT OF NOTING
An act of noting typically consists of two parts:

1. An initial *noticing*, which takes place in a fraction of a second.
2. A period of intently *focusing* on what you noticed. This typically lasts for several seconds, during which you intentionally soak into it and open up to it. This is known as *soaking, penetrating* or *knowing*. Awareness soaks or penetrates the sensory experience. Put another way, we experience the simultaneous arising of the sensory experience and awareness.

So, the practice of noting consists of a sequence of well-defined *noticings* and highly focused *soakings.*

LABELING OPTIONS: SILENT, SPOKEN, WHISPERED
As a general principle, when you're labeling, it's good to note and label at a leisurely pace, allowing about four to six seconds between each labeling.

When you speak labels out loud, use a low, gentle, matter-of-fact, almost-impersonal tone of voice. When you speak them internally (think them), use the same tone in your mental voice.

This leisurely pace allows you to soak in and savour each experience as you note it. The low, gentle, matter-of-fact tone helps you stay in a deeply focused state.

When you label aloud, you have three options for speaking:

- Subvocal speech: mouthing or whispering the words, so they are inaudible to people near you
- Ordinary speech
- Strong (louder-than-usual) speech.

Feel free to shift back and forth among labeling modes as circumstances dictate. If you begin to feel spaced out, unfocused or scattered, immediately shift to a stronger (louder) mode of labeling. Once you get refocused, feel free to return to a softer or more subtle mode.

If you want to keep your labeling practice as simple as possible, choose one mode and stick with it.

When noting and labeling, place no more than five per cent of your attention on the labeling process itself. The other 95 per cent should go into noticing – into the soaking and opening process.

The one exception would be when you find yourself in a period of extreme distraction, when your mind is continually wandering. In this case, use strongly spoken labels, and put 20 per cent or more of your attention into listening to the labels. That way, if the label stream ceases because you have stopped talking, you have instant feedback that lets you know you are losing concentration.

If you are noting without labels and feel yourself getting spaced out or extremely distracted, start to mentally label. If that doesn't help, modulate your mental voice to be more gentle and matter-of-fact, even if that seems artificial and contrived. If that still doesn't make a positive difference, speak the labels out loud in a gentle, matter-of-fact tone. And if you're having further trouble focusing, use strongly spoken labels.

If the effort to speak labels aloud creates uncomfortable internal responses (judgment, resistance, emotion and so on), then label those reactions as *talk*, *feel*, *judge*, etc. Those reactions are actually proof that you're following the procedure correctly. You are going toe-to-toe with unconsciousness.

FREQUENTLY ASKED QUESTIONS ABOUT NOTING AND LABELING WITH SHINZEN

Q: *Labeling is obviously an instance of thinking or talking, so should I note or label it as such? In other words, should I label my labels?*

A: No. Don't label the labels themselves. That would create an infinite regression.

Q: *Noting makes me think more. A lot more. I think about whether or not I'm noting things right. I think about what to do next. I think about thinking about thinking. What should I do?*

A: Just be patient. Those are common initial reactions. Over time, as your mind gets tired of playing games with itself, the noting will become second nature for you and your mind will settle down.

If you need a break from noting, make things simpler: become relaxed, passive and receptive. Just receive the flow of perceptual phenomena from moment to moment, without making any effort to note or label anything. We call this *even coverage*, and it can provide a helpful contrast to the activeness of noting.

Also keep in mind the "three okays" about noting: 1) it's okay to guess, 2) it's okay to miss, and 3) it's okay to be late. Simply do your best and relax into the process.

Q: *It seems that a lot of my labels are just guesses. For example, am I worrying or thinking or imagining or speculating? Is this okay?*

A: Yes. The more you practise, the more precise your labels will become and the more comfortable you'll be with the whole process.

Q: *It seems that my labels often come late, after the fact. For example, I'll note my internal chatter, but won't label it as talk until a second or two later. Is this a problem?*

A: It's not a problem. You are still much more alert than you would be if you weren't noting and labeling the internal chatter of the mind at all.

Q: *A lot of stuff is always going on at once. When I try to label it all, it speeds me up and makes me frenetic. What should I do?*

A: You don't have to notice and label everything. In fact, it's impossible. It's okay to miss things, as long as you really focus on what you do label. Remember, the point is to train your attention in a way that increases concentration, clarity and equanimity.

Q: *Noting, and especially labeling, seem to interfere with what I'm focusing on. I feel like sometimes I can't detect what's really there. What do you recommend?*

A: Actually, you are detecting "what's really there." It's what was there before, plus any change produced by the act of paying attention to it. Remember, in this practice your task is to focus on something specific and then soak in it and savour it. Any sensory experience is valid to focus on, even when that experience has been caused or modified by the act of focusing itself.

Q: *Noting seems to reinforce a strong sense of an "I" that's doing the noting. Is this a problem?*
A: No. It's natural at the beginning. With practice, though, at some point noting goes on autopilot. Just as you can do the complex task of driving a car without needing much of a "driving self," eventually you can quickly and accurately label complex phenomena without needing a "meditating self" who's controlling the process. When that happens, the sense of distance between the person who notices and what is noted disappears.

Q: *I find myself saying "feel" over and over and over again. What's the point? Am I doing something wrong?*
A: Remember that noting is not just noticing and then perhaps applying a label. Each time you note something, you also should intentionally *soak into* it and *open up* to it. As you do this, you intentionally infuse clarity and equanimity into what you note, each time you note. You are doing something very powerful to reprogram the deep mind. You are not wasting your time, even if you just note (and then label) the same banal thing over and over.

This process can be challenging, because initially you may not get any immediate positive feedback to indicate that something is changing deep down. Before you reach this point, the going may be tough and slow. But please keep practising. At some point, you will begin to sense that your awareness is penetrating down into the thing noted, softening and purifying the sensory circuits that lie below. When that happens, you'll start to get immediate tangible feedback that the noting is useful. You also won't be bothered that you're noting (and perhaps also labeling) the same thing over and over.

Q: *Why should I bother noting and labeling at all?*
A: Here are a few of the many reasons:

1. The gentle, matter-of-fact tone you create in your voice as you label can be very powerful. Your own voice can put you into a deep state of reassurance, safety, self-acceptance and equanimity.
2. Noting and labeling allow you to focus on just what's present in the moment. This reduces overwhelm, which in turn reduces suffering.
3. Noting and labeling allow you to break down experiences into manageable parts and to deal with those parts one at a time.

Q: *I really don't like to label. What should I do?*
A: As we said, you don't have to label at all. But if it's a choice between effortful, uncomfortable, unnatural labeling on one hand and being extremely spaced out on the other, go for labeling. With practice, the discomfort will lessen and eventually disappear.

USING NOTING AND LABELING IN UNIFIED MINDFULNESS METHODS

Now that you've become familiar with the basics and perhaps also some of the more subtle points of noting and labeling, it's time to apply these tools to specific Unified Mindfulness methods.

SUMMARY

- Noting and labeling are the raft and oar that will help you skillfully navigate the lake of mindfulness – until you learn (or remember) how to swim.
- Noting involves noticing and then focusing intently but gently on a phenomenon for a few seconds. This is often referred to as awareness *soaking in* or *penetrating* or *opening to* the phenomenon.
- Labeling involves thinking or saying a word or phrase that describes what you are noting.
- Mindfulness, noting and labeling are related. Noting facilitates mindfulness and labeling facilitates noting.
- Labeling supports psychological healing by offering the "wounded warrior" a kind and wise alternative to exacerbating the original wound. Noting and labeling are a healing poultice.

CHAPTER 4

FOCUS ON REST TECHNIQUE

Many people associate the words "meditation" and "mindfulness" almost exclusively with calmness, serenity, peace and relaxation. As you'll learn, there's a lot more that mindfulness training can help us to cultivate. With that said, it's also true that finding, focusing upon and savouring these more tranquil, soft, subtle and silent aspects of our conscious experience – what lies beneath all the activity – are also important parts of it.

THE IMPORTANCE OF REST

As it turns out, focusing on rest is not only enjoyable but also plays a crucial role in the health of our body and mind. Discovering and appreciating restful sensations is a great way to nourish your overall wellbeing – and the Focus on Rest methods can help you do just this.

Rest is vitally important for a human body–mind. Our physical and mental health depend upon restorative sleep cycles – getting enough quality sleep each night. A lack of appropriate levels of sleep has been linked to a wide variety of mental and emotional health challenges, including depression, anxiety and bipolar disorder.

MENTAL HEALTH AND NERVOUS SYSTEM REGULATION

During our waking hours, the ability of our nervous system to access the "rest-digest-restore" functions of the parasympathetic nervous system – rather than getting stuck in a sympathetic "fight-flight-freeze" mode – is also key to overall wellbeing. A regulated nervous system allows a person to adapt to everchanging circumstances without feeling confused or overwhelmed. It provides a sense of confidence, security and healthy agency – a belief in our ability to safely navigate the world.

When the balance between activity and rest – between heightened arousal and relaxation – is disturbed, mental health issues are more likely to arise or be exacerbated. When a person's nervous system becomes dysregulated in this way, feelings of overwhelm and powerlessness are common, along with the experience of being stuck in emotional reactivity.

You may have experienced this yourself, or perhaps you have a friend or a family member whose health is compromised by an inability to "unplug" from a frenzied pace of physical and/ or emotional hyperarousal. A wide range of mental health challenges, including anxiety, trauma, PTSD and depression, are related to this kind of dysregulation of the nervous system.

So, it's vitally important to be able to access the rest-digest-restore functioning of the parasympathetic nervous system, rather than being stuck in overdrive.

FOCUS ON REST CAN RESTORE EMOTIONAL HARMONY

The Unified Mindfulness Focus on Rest technique is a tool not only for cultivating mindfulness – enhancing concentration, clarity and equanimity. It can also help you restore a more balanced relationship between activity and rest, which is likely to have all kinds of positive ripple-effects within your mind and body.

Now, let's look more closely at how shining the light of mindfulness upon restful states works not only to relieve suffering but also to enhance comfort, ease and fulfillment.

THE MIRACLE OF MINDFULNESS

One of the so-called miracles of mindfulness is its capacity to naturally enhance what is wholesome and beneficial within our mind and body, while at the same time tempering, disentangling or dissolving what is harmful. For example, when we direct a beam of mindfulness onto restful places in our mind–body, the comfort, ease, and pleasure inherent in this restfulness tends to deepen. Mindful awareness – like the sun shining upon a flower – allows the restfulness to blossom, to unfold its many layers of quiet joy and easeful contentment. In and of itself, this can be deeply healing.

RESTFUL STATES AND MENTAL HEALTH

When we focus on restful states – characterized by physical relaxation and the *absence* of mental images and mental talk – deep equanimity, concentration and clarity can emerge. With increased clarity and equanimity, emotional reactions are more likely to pass right through us, like an arrow flying through the air with no place to land.

Rather than spinning off into emotional reactivity – a common symptom of mental–emotional disharmony – we remain spacious, clear, balanced, poised. From this clarity, appropriate actions can naturally emerge. In this way, restful states – mindfully enhanced – can help relieve psychological suffering and improve mental health.

Now, let's have a closer look at how becoming mindfully aware of restful states enhances concentration and induces deep levels of equanimity.

RESTFUL STATES ENHANCE CONCENTRATION

Becoming mindfully aware of restful sensations – places in your body–mind that already are at ease – can create a positive feedback loop that strengthens your power to concentrate. How, exactly, does this happen?

Restful sensations are generally pleasant. So, the more that you focus on restfulness, the better you feel. And this then motivates you to give even greater attention to these restful states. The result is that your concentration power is enhanced via this engagement with restful sensations. This elegant and deeply healing feedback loop is one thing that makes the Focus on Rest technique so useful as well as enjoyable.

RESTFUL STATES INDUCE EQUANIMITY

Restful states also create a mental–emotional "container" within which more unpleasant emotions or physical pain can come and go without an added layer of psychological suffering. In other words, the restful states tend to induce equanimity – a nonjudgmental welcoming way of relating to thoughts, feelings and sensations. This way of relating to your mind–body is one of the central goals of mindfulness practice, as a deep acceptance of your inner experience is key to the release of unnecessary suffering.

Most people fail to notice and enjoy the restful states that are present within themselves. The Focus on Rest technique is especially helpful in facilitating this kind of freedom and pleasure. Unified Mindfulness gives you the vocabulary and concepts needed to recognize restful sensations, as well as the tools to more fully welcome and appreciate them.

In later chapters, we'll look at ways to use this technique to help resolve specific mental health issues. But for now, let's get to the nuts-and-bolts of how to actually practise it.

HOW TO PRACTISE FOCUS ON REST

In the following sections, you'll learn how to note and label three "flavours" of rest:

1. Visual rest – the darkness or mottled light/dark pattern behind your eyelids when your eyes are closed
2. Somatic rest – a sense of relaxation in the body
3. Auditory rest – silence in your mind and/or your physical surroundings.

As you note and then allow awareness to fully soak into these restful moments, your body–mind will relax more fully. This can be deeply healing.

SOFTENING EYES: HOW TO NOTE VISUAL REST

When you close your eyes, things typically get dark because you've cut off external light. This darkness – the *absence* of external visual phenomena – can be soothing and restful. But when you close your eyes, there also can be a remnant of brightness. This might be a little external light trickling in through your eyelids, or light, patterns or geometrical shapes associated with your visual mind.

For the visual aspect of the Focus on Rest technique, you'll ignore any colours or geometrical shapes. Instead,

---

you'll focus on one of three very simple and soothing visual experiences behind your closed eyes: darkness; any brightness or grey; and the mottled mixture of darkness and light.

1. Close your eyes. Every few seconds, note the darkness, brightness or mixture of dark and light behind your eyelids. Allow awareness to fully penetrate and soak into the experience.
2. If you choose to also use labels, label whatever you see as *see rest*.
3. If thoughts, feelings or body sensations arise within your awareness, don't try to get rid of them. Instead, simply allow them to be part of the background and gently return your attention to the brightness, darkness or light/dark mixture behind your eyelids.
4. Stay with this practice for 5–10 minutes, or longer if you like.

RELISHING RELAXATION: HOW TO NOTE SOMATIC REST

This will help you to engage with the somatic or bodily aspect of the Focus on Rest technique.

1. Get into a comfortable position, preferably lying down or sitting. Let your body relax.
2. Bring your attention to your body. Notice every place that feels relaxed – an arm, a leg, a foot, your deep belly, your pinky finger or your entire body.
3. If you can't find relaxation anywhere in your body, then simply follow the cycle of your breathing and notice that every time you exhale there is some relaxation,

release or settling that happens naturally – as though your entire body–mind were saying "*ahhh.*"

4. Now focus only on this relaxation, noting instances of physical relaxation every few seconds. If you like, to help you stay focused, use the label *feel rest* every few seconds, speaking the words with a gentle internal or external voice.

5. In this way, note instances of this somatic rest and allow them to become fully soaked in and opened to awareness.

6. Explore this practice for 5–10 minutes, or longer if you like.

ENJOYING SILENCE:
HOW TO NOTE AUDITORY REST

At any moment, you may be able to find instances of auditory rest. This rest can take either of two forms: inner or outer.

Inner auditory rest is an awareness that your mind is quiet, that there is an *absence* of internal dialogue. Another, more subtle form of inner auditory rest is an awareness of the gaps or silent spaces between thoughts.

Outer auditory rest occurs when you can sense an *absence* of sound in one or more spatial directions (including up or down). In other words, your external environment is quiet in one direction or another.

1. When you notice the absence of inner dialogue, gaps between thoughts or an absence of external sound in one or more directions, focus on this quiet. If you like, label it *hear rest.*

2. Note instances of this auditory rest every few seconds and allow them to become soaked in awareness.
3. Continue this practice for 5–10 minutes, longer if you like.

COMBINING THE THREE TYPES OF REST

Once you're comfortable noting and labeling all three types of rest, you can combine the three practices. Let your attention float naturally among them, noting (and perhaps labeling) whichever one you are drawn to in the moment.

If, at a particular moment, you are not able to access one form of rest, simply move to another.

Let yourself enjoy these restful states: fully, deeply and completely.

ABSOLUTE REST: DISCOVERING AND ABIDING AS THE STILL POINT

The Unified Mindfulness techniques introduced in this book – including this chapter's Focus on Rest methods – are mostly about learning to *improve* and more fully *appreciate* "self" and "world." In Part Two, you'll see how these methods can be used to deeply transform and heal specific mental–emotional imbalances, thus improving the quality of your moment-by-moment experience and restoring your capacity to deeply appreciate your human life.

But there's another aspect of Unified Mindfulness that you may wish to explore, which is *transcending* "self" and "world," and accessing a wholly transpersonal and non-phenomenal dimension of experience. The poet TS Eliot alludes to such a dimension as a "still point," and describes its mysterious relationship to the "turning world" – referred to in the poem *Burnt Norton* as a "dance":

"... *Except for the point, the still point,*
There would be no dance, and there is only the dance."*

Unified Mindfulness speaks to this still point – and to the dance – as well, but with different terms: *absolute rest* and *absolute activity*. *Absolute rest* (the "still point") is what arises when something disappears and nothing replaces it. *Absolute activity* (the "dance") is effortless expansion and contraction: the appearance and dissolution of phenomena, moment by moment, without internal resistance. Each of us has the capacity to access and enjoy absolute rest and absolute activity, as fruits of mindful awareness.

We'll return to an in-depth exploration of absolute activity – the dance-partner of absolute rest – in this book's final chapter. But it's worth knowing about absolute rest right from the beginning. What follows is an introduction to this transpersonal and non-phenomenal dimension of rest – known as absolute rest.

I'd encourage you to play with this as frequently as you'd like – to try it now and return to it often. You may be surprised (and perhaps a bit shocked, but in a good way) by what you discover.

---

* Excerpt from "Burnt Norton" in *Four Quartets*, Houghton Mifflin Harcourt: 1968.

A GUIDED EXPLORATION FOR ACCESSING ABSOLUTE REST

Find a comfortable quiet place to sit or lie down. Read the whole exercise in full before beginning.

1. Begin by connecting with an inner smile. Let your lips become wide and full. Let smile energy infuse your eyes, then flow out into all the cells of your body. Smiling gently, say *"Ahh"* as you exhale, relaxing your face, neck and jaw completely. Feel the smile throughout your mind–body.

2. Now close your eyes and imagine that you are blind – that external visual phenomena are no longer part of your experience. With curiosity, investigate how this affects your experience of the world and your sense of self. What's it like to no longer have access to external sights?

3. Next, use your fingers (or a good set of earplugs) to plug your ears. Imagine that you are deaf as well as blind – that both external auditory and visual phenomena are no longer a part of your experience. Investigate how this affects your experience of the world and your sense of self. What's it like to be without external sounds or sights?

4. Then imagine also losing your senses of smell and taste. What do you experience without sight, sound, smell and taste?

5. Next, imagine that your sense of touch, both inside and outside of the body, has disappeared. Now all your human senses have gone. Explore this experience. What is left?

6. In the absence of these five senses, only the mind's phenomena – thoughts, memories, internal images and emotions – remain. Observe these phenomena

for a few minutes. What you'll discover is that most of this mind experience is oriented toward the past or the future. This is the realm of night dreams and daydreams – and of practical and creative thinking.

7. Now continue with this process. Imagine that these thoughts, memories, images and feelings *also* dissolve and do not return. Who and where are you now? What remains? *This* is the still point of *absolute rest* . . . just this simple, pure being-ness; this aware, awake presence; this vibrant stillness. This is "you" in the absence of any sensory or mental content. Rest here for a while, becoming familiar with *this*. Then ask this question: *Here*, in the absence of all sense perception and all thinking, is there a distinction between "me" and "not me" – between "self" and "world"?

Consider the possibility that what can be seen, heard, felt, thought, imagined, or known by the mind is not your true identity. Let go of all these things as they arise, and rest in the vibrant "unknowing" of *this* fertile mystery – *this* sweetly ineffable, unspeakable ease of being.

8. Now reverse the process: one sense at a time, allow the different forms of experience to return. First allow thoughts, images, memories and feelings to return. Then allow touch, then taste, then smell, then hearing and finally vision to return as well. Notice and appreciate how all of these arise and dissolve, weave together and then separate. Notice, too, how all of this creates a moment-by-moment subjective sense of "self" and a moment-by-moment experience of "the world."

* * *

I hope you've enjoyed learning about these Unified Mindfulness Focus on Rest methods – in all their variety. They are inherently valuable and also provide a great foundation for all that follows.

SUMMARY

- The capacity to access restful states is profoundly important for the health of the human body–mind.
- In the Focus on Rest technique, rest comes in three main flavours: *see rest* (darkness, light or a dark/light mixture behind the eyelids), *feel rest* (body relaxation) and *hear rest* (internal or external silence).
- Paying attention to moments of rest enhances their wholesome and beneficial qualities.
- Comfort, ease and pleasure are inherent to restful states in the body–mind.
- From the still-point of *absolute rest* – in the absence of all sense perception and all thinking – it's interesting to ask: is there a distinction between "me" and "not me" – between "self" and "world"?

CHAPTER 5

FOCUS OUT AND FOCUS IN TECHNIQUES

Now that I've introduced the Focus on Rest techniques, it's time to expand your Unified Mindfulness repertoire to include a couple more methods: Focus Out and Focus In. Each of these techniques has the power to support healing and deeply nourish your psychological wellbeing. As such, they're great tools to have on hand.

What makes these mindfulness tools so effective is how they can help you release unnecessary suffering and reveal natural comfort and joy. Let's explore now in a bit more detail how this happens.

UNNECESSARY SUFFERING: THE MIND'S ELABORATE SPIDER-WEB

A good portion of our suffering – the part of it that is truly unnecessary – arises within our mind. All of our worries about the future; our regrets about the past; and theories, hypotheses, conjectures, and beliefs about what is or should be or should not be happening right now – all of these constitute our stories of "self" and "the world." Like a spider spinning an elaborate web, the mind spins out a story, which we often get caught in and suffer from, as a result.

All variety of mental health challenges are associated with these internal stories – with the entangled webs of self-talk, internal images and emotional sensations that generate unnecessary suffering. The Unified Mindfulness techniques you'll learn in this chapter – Focus Out and Focus In – support the untangling of these internal stories and the release of the suffering held within them. That's what makes them so useful for emotional repair.

UNTANGLING AND TRANSPARENCY: HOW FOCUS IN SUPPORTS EMOTIONAL REPAIR

With the Focus In technique, you direct your attention – the beam of mindfulness – *inward* onto the content of your mind. Carefully observing the thoughts, images and feelings that constitute your psychological suffering with a spacious attitude of equanimity, you allow them to untangle – sometimes slowly, sometimes quickly. At other times, you enable them to become so playfully transparent that they cease to be a problem at all.

In either case, the application of this technique can help you restore inner balance, comfort and ease. As the threads of that mind-made spider-web untangle and/or fully dissolve, a natural freedom and vitality can then emerge, quite effortlessly. You're no longer bothered by thoughts, images and feelings – even when they do continue to appear. In other words, they no longer have the power to create psychological suffering. And this is a truly profound discovery!

ANCHORING IN OUR SHARED WORLD: HOW FOCUS OUT NOURISHES MENTAL HEALTH

With the Focus Out technique, you direct your attention *outward* to external sensory phenomena. Immersing yourself fully in the sights, sounds and tactile sensations of your surroundings is another way of extricating yourself from that spider-web of mind-made suffering. Just like the Focus In technique, this focus on external sensations also allows inner reactions – the thoughts, images and feelings of psychological suffering – to naturally untangle. It's just a different (more indirect) way of going about it.

The Focus Out technique also helps you appreciate more deeply and interact more intimately with the beauty of our shared world. Whether the sights, sounds and tactile sensations that you are becoming more mindfully aware of are those of a forest path, a mountain meadow, an urban boulevard or your own kitchen or back yard – it's an opportunity to support mental health and wellbeing in a way that can be truly enjoyable.

Now, let's get to the nuts-and-bolts of how to actually practise these two transformative Unified Mindfulness methods. We'll begin with Focus Out.

HOW TO PRACTISE FOCUSING OUT FOR EXTERNAL FREEDOM AND INTIMACY

In applying the Focus Out technique, you'll be turning your attention *away from* any inner activity (mental images, mental talk and emotional body sensations) that can be a centre of emotional suffering. Instead, you'll turn your attention *toward outer* sensory activity – sights, sounds and non-emotional body sensations (such as heat, cold, texture and external pressure).

With this Focus Out technique, you'll employ three labels:

1. *See out* – for visual phenomena
2. *Hear out* – for auditory phenomena
3. *Feel out* – for physical body sensations

Note: For the basic Focus Out technique, you generally will **not** be noting or labeling tastes or smells – though these sensory modalities may play a role in certain healing applications.

1. Choose a place to practice, either indoors or outside. You can practise the Focus Out technique while you're sitting or lying down (with your eyes open or closed), or walking (with your eyes open, please!).
2. Now, begin to note – become mindfully aware of – external visual experience (sights); external sounds; and a range of physical sensations, such as heat, cold, external pressure and the sensation of clothing making contact with the body, as well as any other non-emotional body sensations.
3. If your eyes are open and your attention flows to external visual experience, note the visual phenomena and label it *see out*. If your attention goes to external sound, note the auditory phenomena and label it *hear out*. If your attention goes to physical body sensations note the sensations and label them *feel out*. If your attention encompasses more than one sensory field, pick one to focus on and label. It does not matter which one you choose.
4. Continue to note and label, at a relaxed, consistent pace (once every few seconds), for 5–10 minutes, or longer if you like.

Note: When applying this method, it's important to avoid any attempt to reject or wish away an emotional reaction, or to wait (with the tension of impatience) for it to go away. Instead, give the emotional reaction permission to stay as long as nature wants it to. Give it permission to come back if it starts to return. Simply continue practising the Focus Out technique, noting and labeling – with gentle yet persistent energy – see out, hear out, and/or feel out – and allowing the sensations to be penetrated and soaked in awareness.

Also, turn away from any thoughts you may have about whether or not the technique is working. Simply refocus on see out, hear out and/or feel out. This allows the strands of psychological suffering to disentangle and dissolve naturally.

COMPLETENESS AND RICHNESS: THE DEEP BENEFITS OF FOCUSING OUT

With practice, as you use the Focus Out technique, the outer world (of sights, sounds and tactile sensations) expands into completeness and richness, while your inner world contracts and settles into rest, stillness and quietude. As a result, emotional suffering, which is rooted in inner dialogue, imagery and emotional reactions, dissolves. This is what makes this Focus Out method so effective for emotional repair.

You can apply the Focus Out technique the moment you realize that you are feeling overwhelmed or entangled in thoughts in a way that's creating suffering. Stay with the technique until the emotional reaction has passed or is no longer a problem. If suffering returns, apply the technique again.

Now, let's explore the other Unified Mindfulness technique covered in this chapter – Focus In – which involves *turning toward* and engaging *directly* with internal talk, mental images and emotional sensations.

HOW TO PRACTISE FOCUSING IN FOR INTERNAL FREEDOM AND INTIMACY

With the Focus In technique, you'll note internal visual experience (images), internal auditory experience (the mind's internal talk or chatter) and emotional sensations in the body.

The three labels you will be employing are:

1. *See in* – for internal images
2. *Hear in* – for internal talk
3. *Feel in* – for emotion experienced in the body

1. Choose a place to practise – indoors is best for beginners. You can practise the Focus In technique while you're sitting or lying down, with your eyes either open or closed.
2. When your attention alights upon an internal image, note this sensory experience; allow it to be fully soaked with awareness; and label it *see in*. If your attention alights on internal talk, note this sensory experience; allow it to be fully soaked with awareness and label it *hear in*. If your attention is drawn to an emotion experienced in the body – such as anger, sadness, fear or joy – note this sensory experience, allow it to be fully soaked with awareness and label it *feel in*.
3. Maintain an even, relaxed rhythm with noting and labeling. Once every three to four seconds is a good rule of thumb.
4. Continue for 5–10 minutes, or longer if you like.

SPACIOUSNESS AND FREEDOM: THE DEEP BENEFITS OF FOCUSING IN

By attending closely – and with a relaxed and spacious equanimity – to patterns of internal thinking (*hearing in*), internal imagery (*seeing in*), and internal emotions (*feeling in*), you can disentangle psychological suffering. You see more clearly how this suffering is created; how it is maintained, protected/ defended, and reproduced; and how it naturally dissolves, moment by moment. This facilitates emotional repair – the unwinding of mental–emotional imbalances – in profound ways.

As you deeply penetrate these strands with awareness, a sense of intimacy, spaciousness and freedom naturally arises. Within this freedom, new choices, new patterns and new possibilities for healing and transformation can emerge.

SUMMARY

- The Focus Out method works by *turning away from* (though not forcibly rejecting) the mind's spider-web of internal dialogue, internal images and emotional feelings – to untangle psychological suffering.
- The three aspects of the Focus Out technique are *see out* (external sights), *hear out* (external sounds) and *feel out* (non-emotional body sensations).
- The Focus In method works by *turning toward* (with spacious equanimity) the mind's spider-web of internal dialogue, internal images and emotional feelings – to untangle psychological suffering.
- The three aspects of the Focus In technique are *see in* (internal imagery), *hear in* (internal dialogue) and *feel in* (emotional body sensations).

- The Unified Mindfulness Focus Out and Focus In
  techniques are powerful tools for diminishing or fully
  dissolving psychological suffering – by untangling the
  mind's spider-web of internal dialogue, internal images
  and emotional body sensations and revealing our natural
  comfort, ease and freedom.

CHAPTER 6

FOCUS ON EVERYTHING TECHNIQUE

In Chapter 4, you learned how to note and label – and enjoyably enhance – restful sensations. In Chapter 5, you explored the options of turning toward or turning away from your mind's spider-web of mental dialogue, internal images and emotional body sensations to extricate yourself from unnecessary suffering.

Now you'll have the opportunity to expand the context of your Unified Mindfulness practice even further, by allowing your attention to alight wherever it wishes:

1. Internally, within the realm of thoughts, images and emotions
2. Externally, within the realm of sounds, sights, smells, tastes and physical body sensations
3. On moments of rest between such experiences.

As you attend to this full spectrum of sensory experience, you will use the labels *see, hear* and *feel* in a universal way, without noting or labeling any distinction between *out, in* or *rest*. This method also includes becoming mindfully aware of smells and tastes – which you will label as *feel.*

77

With the Focus on Everything technique, you allow your attention to roam freely across internal, external and restful experience. Simply note whether a particular instance of sensory experience involves a sight, sound or body sensation, and label it as such. For the most grounding effect, label each experience *out loud* (rather than internally as a silent thought).

The Focus on Everything method is a combination of three other Unified Mindfulness methods: *just see*, *just hear* and *just feel*. Many people alternate among these three techniques until they're comfortable with them all – and then combine them into the Focus on Everything practice. So, I'll begin here with instructions for each of these three "warm-up" methods.

HOW TO PRACTISE *JUST SEE* AND RELISH THE VISUAL SPECTRUM

In the *just see* technique, you'll be mindfully attending to internal, external and restful visual phenomena. This method can be practised either with your eyes closed or open.

1. With eyes closed: if you experience a mental visual image, note this sensory experience, soak it with awareness and label the mental image as *see*. If you have no mental image, focus instead upon the darkness or brightness behind your eyelids. Note this as a restful visual state, soak it with awareness and also label this absence of internal image as *see*.
2. With eyes open: let your attention be drawn to either external sights or mental images. Gently focus on, note and soak into the visual experience and label it *see*.
3. When labeling, do so at a moderate pace and use a gentle tone. If you get distracted by a different sense, gently return to the visual field, noting and labeling *see*.

HOW TO PRACTISE *JUST HEAR* AND EXPLORE THE AUDITORY SPECTRUM

1. With your eyes either open or closed, let your attention be drawn to external sounds, mental chatter or silence.
2. Every few seconds, label your experience as *hear*, indicating that you are gently focusing on, noting and soaking into either sound or silence.
3. If you become distracted by a different sense, gently return your attention to noting and labeling *hear*.

HOW TO PRACTISE *JUST FEEL* AND ENJOY THE SOMATIC SPECTRUM

The somatic spectrum includes both physical sensations as well as emotional body sensations.

1. With your eyes either open or closed, direct your attention to the field of your physical body.
2. Every few seconds, note a physical or emotional body sensation; allow that body experience to be fully penetrated and soaked with awareness and label the experience *feel*.
3. If you become distracted by a different sense, gently return your attention to noting and labeling *feel*.

HOW TO PRACTISE FOCUS ON EVERYTHING AND RANGE FREELY

The Focus on Everything technique combines *just see*, *just hear* and *just feel*. You allow your attention to roam across all your senses – as well as among internal sensations, external sensations and rest.

With the Focus on Everything practice, you cannot be "distracted" from one sensation by another. Instead, this movement is seen as a natural flow that does not need to be interrupted or corrected, simply noted and labeled as what it is.

1. Allow your attention to float across whatever sense (sight, hearing, physical sensations, emotions, smell or taste) and whatever specific sensations you are naturally drawn to in the moment.
2. Note each sensation; allow the experience to be fully soaked with awareness and label the experience *see*, *hear* or *feel* accordingly.
3. Allow your attention to stay with one sense or sensation or to float across a variety of them – whatever feels most natural, enjoyable and/or useful to you.
4. Be genuinely curious – in a wholly innocent and childlike way – about this moment-by-moment sensory experience. Allow yourself to appreciate how amazing it is to witnesses this everchanging kaleidoscope of sensory phenomena!

HOW FOCUS ON EVERYTHING SUPPORTS PSYCHOLOGICAL WELLBEING

All of the psychological benefits of the Focus on Rest, Focus Out and Focus In methods are at play in the Focus on Everything technique. Contacting restful sensations is deeply nourishing. And embracing internal phenomena (thoughts, images, emotions) and external phenomena (sights, sounds, tastes, smells, physical body sensations) with mindful awareness supports the untangling of the threads of sensory experience which, in their contracted, congealed, tangled state had become the source of unnecessary psychological suffering.

As such, the Unified Mindfulness Focus on Everything method can be a valuable tool for emotional repair and the unveiling of our natural peace, joy and freedom.

SUMMARY

- The Focus on Everything technique is a combination of *just feeling* (physical and emotional body sensations, including taste, smell and bodily rest), *just seeing* (external and internal sights or visual rest), and *just hearing* (external and internal sounds, including mental talk or auditory rest).
- The labels used in the Focus on Everything technique are simple and familiar – *see*, *hear* and *feel*.
- These labels are applied to experiences coming from all locations, internal and external, as well as to the state of rest between (and as the background of) such experiences.
- In the Focus on Everything technique attention floats freely, guided by interest, enthusiasm, curiosity and fascination with sensory experience.

CHAPTER 7

NURTURE THE POSITIVE

If you've been progressing through this book chapter by chapter – from front to back – your Unified Mindfulness toolkit now includes four truly wonderful methods: Focus on Rest, Focus Out, Focus In and Focus on Everything. Together, these mindfulness techniques can help you access and enhance deeply healing restful states, and effectively disentangle threads of sensory experience that have been bothering you, causing unnecessary suffering.

The next Unified Mindfulness technique I'll share with you – here in this chapter – is Nurture the Positive. This method involves *intentionally creating* positive internal thoughts, images and emotions, rather than simply noting and labeling what arises.

It's best to explore this Nurture the Positive method only once you've become adept at the previous Unified Mindfulness techniques of simply noting and labeling what is arising. But once you do feel comfortable and confident with those methods – with accessing restful experience with Focus on Rest; untangling threads of sensory experience with Focus In and Focus Out; and letting your attention range freely in Focus on Everything – then you're ready to enter the territory of *intentionally creating* positive thoughts, images and emotions.

As you practise nurturing the positive, you'll learn to activate your creative energy in the form of visualizations and consciously chosen self-talk. You'll also learn how the simple act of smiling has the power to generate positive emotions and can radically transform the biochemistry of your mind–body. This feedback loop between how you feel and your brain's biochemistry is interesting and can be used to support emotional repair and psychological wellness.

THE LINK BETWEEN BIOCHEMISTRY AND MOOD

You may have heard of a category of hormones (the body's chemical messengers) known as "feel-good hormones." As their nickname implies, these hormones – serotonin, dopamine, oxytocin and endorphins – are associated with feeling good, with an enhancement of mood. They can generate a range of positive emotions: feelings of happiness, trust, satisfaction, excitement and even euphoria.

These "feel-good hormones" are not only hormones but also neurotransmitters: chemical messengers that carry information from one neuron (brain cell) to another. The main difference between hormones and neurotransmitters is where they act within the body. Hormones travel through the bloodstream to different organs and tissues, while neurotransmitters function in the brain and central nervous system. The "feel-good hormones" work in both ways.

MEET THE "FEEL-GOOD HORMONES"

While these four hormones are classified together as "feel-good hormones," each also has some unique characteristics.

- **Serotonin** is a mood stabilizer that's associated with enhanced feelings of happiness and wellbeing. Along with stabilizing a person's mood, it can help decrease feelings of worry, concern or anxiety and is also involved in learning and memory functions. The release of serotonin is triggered naturally by regular things you do – such as getting a good night's sleep, taking a walk outside in the sunshine, spending time in nature or any other activities that reduce your stress levels.

- **Dopamine** creates feelings of pleasure and plays a motivational role in the brain's reward system. Dopamine is released when you're doing something that you genuinely enjoy. This might be eating a delicious meal, listening to your favourite music, getting a massage or playing tennis with a friend. The release of dopamine provides the body–mind with feelings of wellbeing and motivates you to continue to engage in activities that you enjoy and do well.

- **Oxytocin** is also nicknamed the "love hormone" or "cuddle hormone" because it is associated with loving touch, trust and human bonding in close relationships. The release of oxytocin is correlated with a decrease in anxiety and an increase in the level of overall satisfaction with one's life. Oxytocin also stimulates the release of serotonin and dopamine.

- **Endorphins** help reduce feelings of pain and support the body in more effectively dealing with stress. Endurance athletes often describe an "endorphin rush" or an "endorphin high" that they get when pushing their body to the point of extreme discomfort or pain. The release of endorphins creates a brief euphoria that at least temporarily relieves the painful sensations. While endorphins are released in response to stressful or painful situations, they're also released during other activities such as moderate-intensity exercise, eating or having sex.

As you can see from these brief descriptions, there are certain life activities that help trigger the "feel-good hormones." And, as it turns out, the simple act of smiling is one of these activities! Smiling tends to lift a person's mood and affects brain biochemistry in ways that are supportive of mental health and happiness.

HOW SMILING AFFECTS YOUR BRAIN

Simply put, smiling invites the activation of all four of the "feel-good hormones." This feel-good jamboree in your brain will tend to lift your mood, relax your body, relieve stress and motivate wholesome activities.

As mentioned above, the release of endorphins acts as a 100-per-cent natural pain reliever – your body's own internal opiates. And the release of serotonin via your smile acts as a natural mood enhancer – a 100-per-cent natural antidepressant that doesn't require a prescription and has no negative side effects. It comes free of charge from your body's own internal pharmacy.

And all of this is instigated by a simple smile!

THE SHADOW SIDE OF SMILING

Before getting into the nuts-and-bolts of how to practise the Unified Mindfulness Nurture the Positive technique – and how to invite a healing inner smile – it's worth acknowledging a potential shadow side of smiling.

Sometimes, "faking it until you make it" is a legitimate strategy, and this can be true of smiling. But forced or insincere smiles may also be a symptom of individual or intrapersonal dysfunction that is best addressed as such. For example:

- In families that have a low tolerance for the expression of negative or difficult emotions, children (and parents too) may use smiling to mask what they're really feeling – to avoid being honest about their authentic feelings.
- In certain abusive relationships, smiling may become a gesture of submission.
- Sometimes smiles are associated with discomfort or uncertainty about what to do in a difficult situation. They can be used as an escape to avoid facing the difficulty directly.

In most cases, however, smiling is a really good thing!

THE POWER OF YOUR SMILE

It might seem strange, and even a bit awkward, to *intentionally* smile. But we can approach it as a yoga posture for the lips and mouth. Like other yoga postures, smiling promotes the wellbeing of the body–mind and creates positive, wholesome, harmonious results.

Smiling activates the release of neuropeptides that help reduce stress. As mentioned previously, it also increases levels of feel-good neurotransmitters such as serotonin, dopamine and endorphins. Serotonin acts as an anti-depressant and endorphins are a natural pain reliever. Smiling is genuinely medicinal in the very best way! And all this without a single negative side effect.

As meditation teacher Thich Nhat Hanh has observed, "Sometimes your joy is the source of your smile, but sometimes your smile can be the source of your joy." It works both ways. The mind affects the body and the body also affects mind – in a kind of tangled hierarchy.

To help you get started with this yoga of the mouth, here's a guided exploration that I hope you'll enjoy.

GENTLE SMILE: A DEEPLY NOURISHING EXPLORATION

Don't think of this as a formal technique. Just consider it something to explore and play with.

When the spirit moves you, wherever you happen to be, stop and just smile – gently and warmly for several seconds. Then, for a few seconds after that, note the effects of the smile on your mind–body. Does it shift your experience in some way: physically, mentally and/or emotionally?

As a fun variation, alternate smiling with frowning or grimacing, and note what you feel in your mind–body with each facial expression.

Though a smile may start at your lips, you can allow its energy to spread and flow up and out, into your eyes and beyond. Smiling eyes emanate warmth, clarity and openness.

To help your eyes become conduits for smile energy, try playfully moving them around a bit, with your head remaining still. Move them from left to right and back; then up and down; then in circles, first clockwise, then counterclockwise. Then smile again – with your eyes as much as your lips.

With practice, you can let smile energy expand and ripple out even further, until it flows throughout your mind–body, enlivening every cell. Practise and play, allowing your whole body – every organ, every cell, all the bones and muscles – to smile. Let your body become warm, soft, vibrant and at ease with smile energy.

As you'll discover, adding a gentle smile to any of the mindfulness techniques in this book can make the experience more enjoyable, more powerful and more healing. And this is especially true of Nurture the Positive.

HOW TO PRACTISE NURTURE THE POSITIVE

There are three components to the Unified Mindfulness technique Nurture the Positive. These are *see good*, *hear good* and *feel good*.

See good

1. This aspect of nurturing the positive involves visualizing yourself acting in a positive way or abstaining from a potentially harmful action. For example, if you want to stop smoking, you might create a mental image of being out to dinner with friends and choosing *not* to smoke around them. Or, if you want to be more confident in your interactions with someone, visualize yourself with this person, at ease and comfortable in a pleasant situation.
2. Once you've chosen an appropriate visual image, sit quietly whenever you'd like – first thing in the morning and right before bed are especially excellent – and bring this image to mind.
3. Smile gently and notice the effect of holding this image in mind.
4. Continue for 5–10 minutes, or longer if you like.

Hear good

1. This aspect of nurturing the positive involves mentally repeating an uplifting, positive and *realistic* statement – for example, *I deserve to be treated well in relationships* or *I can stick up for my friend as she faces this difficulty*. This can be a powerful tool to counteract negative messages and toxic self-talk that run on autopilot in our subconscious minds.

2. Once you've chosen an uplifting positive statement that is appropriate to your situation, sit quietly whenever you'd like – first thing in the morning and right before bed are especially excellent – and mentally repeat this statement.
3. Smile gently and notice the effect of repeating this positive, nourishing, uplifting statement.
4. Continue for 5–10 minutes, or longer if you like.

Feel good
This aspect of nurturing the positive involves generating positive emotional sensations in your body. Here are some ideas:

1. Smile gently (as described on page 88).
2. Focus on an area of your body that already feels relaxed or pleasant.
3. Think of a positive image, idea or experience – the laugh of a child, the scent of a flower, the hug of a friend – and then focus on the positive body sensations which the image engenders.
4. Actually have a positive *feel good* experience in your waking life – tickle that child, smell that flower or hug that friend – and note the positive body sensations you feel as a result.

In later chapters, it will become even more clear how useful nurturing the positive can be for facilitating emotional repair and supporting overall psychological wellbeing within the context of my UMED Process.

SUMMARY

- Nurture the Positive includes *see good, hear good* and *feel good.*
- Nurture the Positive involves intentionally creating positive thoughts, images and emotional sensations in the body – rather than simply noting and labeling what arises.
- Smiling works like yoga of the mouth. It has powerfully uplifting effects on the mind–body, increasing the production of feel-good neurotransmitters.
- The feedback loop between how you feel and your brain's biochemistry can be used to support emotional repair and psychological wellness.

CHAPTER 8

SELF-IMAGING

In the previous chapter, you learned the three components of nurturing the positive: *see good, hear good* and *feel good*. Now, we're going to combine these three into a powerfully creative variation of the Nurture the Positive practice called Self-Imaging.

Like *see good, hear good* and *feel good*, the Self-Imaging technique uses imagination and visualization. The difference is that you're now going to use all three of these together to skillfully revise your self-image. This is a more complex – yet very effective – way of nurturing the positive. It can also be great fun.

WHAT IS A SELF-IMAGE?

Our self-image is comprised of how we see ourselves, think about ourselves and feel about ourselves. There's a human body that we see in the mirror, which forms part of our self-image. But there is also an *internal* image that we have of ourselves: how we picture, think about and feel about ourselves. And each component of our self-image is open to revision.

One way to revise our self-image is to playfully replace it with an inspiring ideal, archetype or avatar – one that symbolizes qualities we wish to embody more fully. This is the heart of the self-imaging technique.

YOUR NEW ROLE: HOW TO CHOOSE AN ARCHETYPE, AVATAR OR IDEAL

How do you go about choosing a new role to imagine yourself inhabiting? The possibilities are nearly infinite and should be guided mostly by your own interest and enthusiasm. What lights your fire? What feels most deeply inspiring, nourishing, uplifting, energizing, intriguing or compelling? Go with that! For some general guidance, I would suggest choosing your new role (to use in this Self-Imaging practice) from one of these categories:

1. **An ideal: something you aspire to.** You might envision yourself as a statesman giving an inspiring speech; or as an opera star singing a rousing finale; or as a saxophonist performing a great riff; or as a basketball player sailing through the air for a dunk.

2. **An archetype: the embodiment of a quality.** You might visualize yourself as Saint Francis, the embodiment of gentleness; as Rumi, the embodiment of mystical ecstasy; as Mother Teresa, the embodiment of kindness; as Krishna, the embodiment of divine power and playfulness; as the Dalai Lama, the embodiment of compassion; as Mother Mary, the embodiment of love; or simply yourself, as the embodiment of any of these archetypes.

3. **An avatar: a deity or realized being in bodily form.** You might imagine yourself as an incarnate divine teacher – or anyone whom you relate to as a spiritual guide. (The word *avatar* also refers to an icon on your computer screen that represents a particular person. In a similar fashion, you are representing yourself in a new way through your visualization.)

4. **A meaningful symbol.** A geometric shape (for example, a circle, sphere or star); a celestial body (such as the Sun, the Moon or a comet); a mountain (like Mount Kailash, Mount

Fuji, Mount Olympus, Arunachala or Mount Everest); a
sacred or significant place (for example, Machu Picchu,
the Red Rocks of Sedona, or the southernmost point of
Key West); an animal (such as a lion, an eagle, a dolphin, a
hummingbird or a horse); or even a natural phenomenon
(like a redwood tree, a meadow or a deep, wide river).
There are endless possibilities.

Once again, any image that feels uplifting, inspiring, nourishing,
empowering, wholesome or healing is perfect for this Self-
Imaging practice.

Roles to **avoid** are those you associate with negative
emotions, actions or mind-states, such as cruelty, ignorance,
vengeance or disempowerment.

Once you've done the "prep work" of choosing an inspiring
new role to inhabit, you're ready to engage with the full Self-
Imaging technique.

HOW TO PRACTISE SELF-IMAGING

The Self-Imaging method combines the three components
of Nurture the Positive: see good, hear good and feel good.
There are five basic steps.

1. Choose an ideal, archetype, avatar or meaningful
   symbol whose qualities you admire. (See opposite for
   general guidelines and inspiration on how to make
   this choice.)
2. Using your imagination and powers of visualization,
   replace your current self-image with an internal visual
   image of that ideal, archetype, avatar or symbol. In
   your mind's eye, and in as much detail as possible,
   picture yourself becoming the shape, size, colour,

texture, pattern and movement of your chosen ideal, archetype, avatar or symbol.

3. Replace your usual mental self-talk with words or sounds associated with your chosen ideal, archetype, avatar or symbol. What kind of sounds does this new "you" make? What language (human or otherwise) do they speak? Do they whisper or sing or chant? Do they speak in prose or poetry? What do they say? Let these new words, sounds and ways of speaking resonate through your inner and outer hearing like the sweetest of lullabies.

4. Create positive feelings in your body – such as comfort, joy, confidence, courage, enthusiasm or awe – that you associate with this ideal. Let yourself *feel* what it's like to fully inhabit this role. With passion and playfulness, do your best to *embody* the emotional sensations that you associate with your ideal, archetype, avatar or symbol.

5. Continue to enjoy (with a gentle smile) these positive emotions rippling through your body–mind – even as the images and mental talk dissolve. As the imagined form and sounds dissolve, can you tune into and appreciate a subtle residue or "perfume" of positive feelings? Welcome these and enjoy them for as long as they last.

The Self-Imaging technique lets you "try on" a completely different – and, perhaps, radically upgraded – self-image. It's like an actor playing a role. It's an experiment that can be powerfully transformative – catalyzing healing and revealing deep insight.

Don't worry too much about doing this right – just do your best in a relaxed and playful way. Though I've used the word *visualize*, you don't have to focus only (or at all) on the visual.

Feel free to imagine using any or all of your other senses. With practice, you'll become more and more adept at self-imaging.

SELF-IMAGING IS A MINDFULNESS METHOD

It's important to remember that Self-Imaging is a mindfulness method: an internal, mental practice that uses your powers of imagination and visualization in very precise ways.

It's not about spacing out and fantasizing or *actually* dressing up like an actor in a play, or creating and enacting a real-life alter ego. And it's not about pretending to be someone you're not – though it might feel a bit like this at times.

Instead, Self-Imaging is a brief, in-the-moment mental exercise in which you visualize yourself in a positive role. This includes the creation of positive emotions, which you then note (and perhaps also label), exactly as you would in any other mindfulness practice.

SELF-IMAGING AND PSYCHOLOGICAL WELLBEING

The Self-Imaging technique can be deeply beneficial for almost everyone. It exercises our imagination in ways that support the process of replacing negative limiting beliefs with more empowering beliefs – which is a component of the UMED Process (which you'll be introduced to in Part Two). A radically upgraded self-image can help you become more relaxed, content, happy and emotionally healthy.

Creative self-imaging also supports the insight that our psychological self is fluid, impermanent and everchanging – that it is constructed moment by moment. To understand this deeply is to dislodge the very lynchpin of psychological suffering and open the way to unconditioned peace, joy and freedom.

One notable exception would be people diagnosed with dissociative identity disorder (DID) or any of the psychotic disorders. In such cases, this or any other mindfulness technique is best employed only under the supervision of a psychiatrist. (For an example of a successful collaboration between a mindfulness guide and a psychiatrist, see the case study in Chapter 2, page 40.)

But for most people, playfully replacing your current self-image with a radically upgraded self-image can nourish your creativity, support mental–emotional wellbeing and potentially reveal profound insights into the ultimate nature of "self" and "world."

EXAMPLE: USING SELF-IMAGING TO NOURISH MENTAL HEALTH

Here's an example of how the five steps of the Self-Imaging method might be employed in the service of emotional repair and the enhancement of mental health.

Riley has been feeling increasingly fearful and timid. She decides to use Self-Imaging to become more courageous.

1. To begin, she chooses the role of a vibrantly healthy and powerful lioness. To Riley, a lioness also symbolizes courage – which makes it a perfect choice to help her access her own.
2. Riley then visualizes herself as a lioness, replacing her human body with the body of a lioness. In her mind, she senses her thick fur, her long tail and her sharp claws.
3. Riley also replaces her typical mental self-talk (*I don't have the strength to accomplish anything important*) with

a lion's ferociously confident roar and this thought: *I am powerful and courageous.*

4. Riley generates feelings of confidence, power, energy and enthusiasm. As these feelings arise in her body, she notes them and labels them as *feel* or *feel good.*

5. After 30–60 seconds, Riley allows the mental images and self-talk to dissolve. But she continues to enjoy (with a gentle smile) the positive emotional sensations that linger. These positive feelings soak into her body and naturally uplift her mind.

Now that you've become comfortable with Self-Imaging and the other Unified Mindfulness methods described in Part One, you will be able to apply these methods to the healing of specific psychological conditions – with the help of my Unified Mindfulness Exposure and Desensitization (UMED) Process, which is the focus of Part Two.

SUMMARY

- Self-Imaging is a combination of the three techniques of Nurture the Positive: *see good, hear good* and *feel good.*
- In the Self-Imaging method, you replace your current self-image with a radically upgraded self-image – one that helps you become more peaceful, happy, empowered and emotionally healthy.
- Self-Imaging is an internal process that supports the creation of positive emotional sensations. Once these good feelings have been activated, the internal images and self-talk are allowed to dissolve – but a subtle residue or "perfume" of positive feeling often remains, to be beneficially savoured.

PART TWO

MINDFULNESS AND EXPOSURE THERAPY – A FORTUITOUS COLLABORATION

Now that you've become comfortable with the Unified Mindfulness methods described in Part One, you can apply these methods to the transformation and healing of specific psychological conditions – with the help of my Unified Mindfulness Exposure and Desensitization (UMED) Process. This innovative process combines Unified Mindfulness methods with exposure and desensitization tools and cognitive behavioural techniques to facilitate emotional repair and enhance overall wellbeing.

Chapter 9 introduces the basics of exposure and desensitization therapy – what it is and how it works. Here you'll also find a wealth of helpful tips and strategies for successfully engaging with each aspect of the UMED Process.

In **Chapter 10** you will learn the six basic steps of the UMED Process. With practice, you'll understand how to skillfully combine various Unified Mindfulness methods with exposure and desensitization protocols to support psychological healing.

Chapters 11–15 present inspiring scenarios drawn from my mindfulness-centred psychotherapy practice that show the UMED Process in action, helping to resolve anxiety, panic, addictions, obsessive-compulsive disorder (OCD) and trauma.

Here you'll get to see how each step of the UMED Process is applied and how they work together to facilitate emotional repair and enhance mental health.

Chapter 16 discusses alternate routes – possible ways to lengthen, shorten or revise the steps of the UMED Process, giving you the flexibility to respond with greatest intelligence and sensitivity to your own or a client's unique circumstances.

CHAPTER 9

UNIFIED MINDFULNESS EXPOSURE AND DESENSITIZATION PROCESS – ORIGINS AND INTRODUCTION

Now that you've had some practice with the basic Unified Mindfulness techniques, you've begun to experience how they can reduce or dissolve mental and emotional suffering. And this, already, is wonderful!

But Unified Mindfulness has even more to offer. With Unified Mindfulness methods as my foundation, I've developed the Unified Mindfulness Exposure and Desensitization (UMED) Process to help people heal more deeply and completely from many types of psychological problems, such as anxiety, panic, impulse control disorders, addiction, obsessive compulsive disorder and trauma. The UMED Process powerfully supports emotional repair and helps people get their lives back on track.

The UMED Process emerged out of several years of experimentation in the context of my psychotherapy practice – along with what turned out to be a very auspicious "accident."

A FORTUITOUS COLLABORATION

In 2014 I received training in Eye Movement Desensitization and Reprocessing (EMDR) – a therapeutic modality used primarily to help resolve trauma. It's in this context that I first learned about exposure and desensitization protocols. (More on these protocols below.)

EMDR makes use of bilateral stimulation as a tool for fully activating both sides of the brain to support the desensitization process and facilitate the resolution of traumatic memories. And this, in turn, helps to promote emotional regulation.

Bilateral stimulation means that the two sides of the body are stimulated one after the other, back-and-forth. In the classic form of EMDR, the client is instructed to think about a traumatic event while simultaneously moving their eyes back and forth, left to right. This eye movement is guided by the movement of their therapist's finger or the back-and-forth flashing of a light-bar. The idea is that, over time, this kind of eye movement (which mimics the REM sleep cycle) helps the person's brain reprocess the memories so they can more fully heal from the traumatic experience.

But eye movements are not the only type of bilateral stimulation. Other methods include having the client tap with their right hand on their left knee (or shoulder), then their left hand on their right knee (or shoulder), back-and-forth. Another way is for them to use headphones to listen to music, chimes or audio tones that alternate from their left to right ears.

I used a pair of plastic pulsators (aka tappers or buzzers) to provide bilateral stimulation. My clients would hold one of these in each of their hands and the pulsators would provide alternating mild vibrations, back-and-forth between their two hands.

However, when I first began offering EMDR sessions to my clients, I wasn't all that thrilled with the results. My clients' attention seemed to be all over the place. They were perpetually distracted and unable to concentrate during the process.

I spoke to a friend – a professional colleague who also was familiar with mindfulness – about these difficulties in applying the EMDR protocol. He said, "Why don't you try incorporating some mindfulness methods?"

So then, as an experiment and following my intuition, I began employing mindfulness techniques for desensitization, along with the hand-held buzzers. As I made this transition, I started to have much more success applying the EMDR protocol. The mindfulness-centred desensitization along with bilateral stimulation (via the buzzers) seemed to be working very well.

Specifically, teaching my clients how to cultivate equanimity in relation to the triggered emotions, thoughts, internal images and/or physical sensations allowed the desensitization process to unfold with much greater precision and efficiency.

One day, right as I was beginning a session, I realized that the buzzers were broken. This meant that I would need to improvise. I could have employed another means of bilateral stimulation – for example having my client tap back-and-forth on their knees or shoulders or using my finger to guide a back-and-forth eye movement.

But since I already had begun experimenting (quite successfully) with incorporating Unified Mindfulness methods into the EMDR sessions, I decided to skip the bilateral stimulation and instead use a mindfulness technique alone to facilitate the desensitization process.

And, well, let's just say that this mechanical failure (the broken pulsators) turned out to be quite fortuitous! I discovered that Unified Mindfulness techniques worked very well on their own to help clients process the thoughts, feelings and images that arose within the exposure and desensitization process. And I was liberated from the belief that bilateral stimulation was an indispensable element of the desensitization process.

The collaboration between exposure therapy and mindfulness methods was supremely effective. By 2016 I had transitioned fully to this way of working – and the UMED Process had fully taken shape.

MAIN COMPONENTS OF THE UMED PROCESS

The three main components of the UMED Process are:

1. Unified Mindfulness methods
2. Exposure and desensitization tools
3. Cognitive behavioural techniques.

You've already learned (in Chapters 4–8) several powerful Unified Mindfulness techniques: Focus on Rest, Focus Out, Focus In, Focus on Everything, Nurture the Positive and Self-Imaging. If you're feeling comfortable with these mindfulness methods, you'll be able to apply them effectively within the UMED Process.

The cognitive behavioural component of the UMED Process includes identifying negative beliefs and replacing them with more empowering beliefs. It can also include identifying destructive behaviours and replacing them with more nourishing and constructive ways of acting. I'll return to this topic later, along with some tips on how to identify negative beliefs.

But what about exposure and desensitization? What is this, and what makes its collaboration with Unified Mindfulness techniques so effective?

Simply put, "exposure and desensitization" refers to a psychotherapeutic protocol – a set of skills/tools designed to support healing – that are used in several therapeutic modalities. As mentioned, it is central to eye movement desensitization and reprocessing (EMDR) protocols for the resolution of trauma. It is also used in exposure and response prevention (ERP) therapy for the treatment of obsessive-compulsive disorder. And it is employed sometimes within the context of cognitive behavioural therapy (CBT). The application of exposure and desensitization tools is also known simply as exposure therapy.

WHAT IS EXPOSURE THERAPY?

The overall goal of exposure therapy is to help a person confront and overcome their fears by gradually exposing them, within a safe environment, to the things they are afraid of.

From your own experience, you may have noticed that when you're afraid of something – for example, a specific activity, object, person or situation – you tend to avoid it. So, if you're afraid of flying you might avoid traveling or choose to take a train or bus instead. If you're afraid of snakes, you may avoid hiking in places where you might encounter one. If you're afraid of a particular person, you may avoid going places where you're likely to cross paths with them.

And in the short term, this avoidance might make sense (especially if there's a potentially real danger) and keep the fear at bay. It might seem like an intelligent strategy. But in the long term such avoidance can exacerbate the fear, and make it even worse. In addition, irrational fears can prevent you from pursuing cherished goals and fully embracing your life.

In such situations, exposure therapy – exposure and desensitization protocols – can help break the pattern of avoidance and fear. Within a safe environment, a person is gradually exposed to the things they fear and avoid. Over time, this repeated exposure to the feared objects, activities or situations helps reduce fear and decrease avoidance. In other words, the person gradually becomes *desensitized* to what they had previously feared. The object, activity, person or situation no longer bothers them. The fearful sensations are replaced by feelings of equanimity, indifference or even boredom.

Exposure therapy has been scientifically proven to be effective (on its own or in conjunction with other modalities) in the resolution of a range of psychological problems, including phobias, panic disorder, social anxiety disorder, generalized anxiety disorder, post-traumatic stress disorder and obsessive-compulsive disorder. If you or someone you know suffers from one of these conditions, an exposure and desensitization process may be deeply beneficial – potent medicine to help resolve the issue. It could help you or your loved one feel a lot better and enjoy life more fully.

EXPOSURE AND DESENSITIZATION BASICS

Now, let's consider in a bit more detail how exposure and desensitization protocols work.

In the section above, I asked you to consider whether you've had the experience of stridently avoiding something that you're afraid of. This is one way of relating to things that scare us.

But you may also have had the experience of being afraid of something but then discovering that the fear became less intense over time, as you continued to encounter the feared object, person, activity or situation. For example (recalling one of the examples above), you might have been afraid of flying but then discovered that the more flights you took, the easier it got. After a couple years of air travel – for work, or to visit friends or family or to take vacations – the fear of flying was completely gone.

Or you might have had a mortal fear of public speaking but continued to book public speaking events and discovered that each time it became easier – until your anxiety around public speaking had become minimal or perhaps even disappeared completely.

These examples illustrate how the exposure and desensitization process works: the more that you do something that you feel afraid of doing or the more you are exposed to an object or person that you feel afraid of – and you notice that nothing terrible has happened – the less afraid you become. Without these fears hampering your thoughts, words and actions you can inhabit your life more fully.

EXPOSURE THERAPY WITHIN THE UMED PROCESS

While exposure therapy was originally developed as a way of helping people overcome fear and anxiety, I now employ exposure and desensitization protocols, within the UMED Process, for a broad range of mental–emotional disturbances that include but also go beyond fear and anxiety. Frustration, craving, grief, guilt, disappointment, jealousy, resentment and anger are just some examples of emotions that, in my experience, can be skillfully released using exposure and desensitization techniques.

I also apply the exposure and desensitization protocol to physical sensations that may accompany disturbing thoughts or emotions. Because I'm using Unified Mindfulness methods to facilitate the desensitization process, any internal or external phenomena that has been triggered can be skillfully addressed – because the Unified Mindfulness system includes methods for every aspect of our human experience. Internal images, mental dialogue and emotions, as well as external sights, sounds or physical sensations, can be equally resolved into equanimity with a mindfulness-enhanced exposure and desensitization process.

EQUANIMITY AS A KEY TO DESENSITIZATION

It is the cultivation of mindfulness-based equanimity within the desensitization process that sets the UMED Process apart from more traditional applications of exposure and desensitization.

As we've discussed at length in previous chapters, equanimity is a key component (along with concentration and clarity) of mindfulness. Applying Unified Mindfulness techniques to the disturbing thoughts, images, emotions and/or body sensations that are triggered within the exposure and desensitization process allows emotional reactivity to be replaced by equanimity in a most direct and efficient way. This is what makes the collaboration between Unified Mindfulness techniques and exposure and desensitization protocols so brilliantly effective.

Now, let's explore the exposure and desensitization process in a bit more detail, so you can feel comfortable and confident engaging with this powerful therapeutic process.

WAYS OF SAFELY FACING YOUR FEARS

When using exposure and desensitization protocols, there are several ways that a person may – within the safe environment of a healing session – come face-to-face with what they fear.

- They may be supported in **directly facing** a feared object or activity. For example, a person who is afraid of snakes might be encouraged to pick up and hold an actual living snake.

- Alternatively, the person may be encouraged to **vividly imagine** the feared object. So, for example, the person who is afraid of snakes might imagine holding a snake or encountering one in their garden.

- Another way to facilitate exposure to a feared object or situation is with the assistance of **video** or **virtual reality technology**. For example, someone with a fear of snakes might watch a video or take a virtual hike through a jungle filled with all variety of snakes using a VR headset that simulates all the sights, sounds, smells and tactile sensations of a snake-filled jungle – all from within the comfort and safety of their therapist's office.

- Finally, a person may be supported in deliberately **creating the physical sensations** (or tastes and smells) associated with a feared object or situation – for the purpose of learning that the feared sensations themselves are not dangerous. So, someone whose fear of snakes is associated with a racing heartbeat might be encouraged to ride an exercise bike or treadmill to deliberately raise their heartrate in order to become more comfortable with this physical sensation and learn that it can be safe for them to experience it.

In each of these cases, what's known as a **trigger** – a mental image, situation or experience that *activates* the challenging emotional disturbance – is applied to intentionally expose the person to the feared object, activity, situation or person. With repeated exposure, the fear (or other emotional disturbance) gradually subsides.

In the UMED Process, Unified Mindfulness techniques are applied to whatever thoughts, feelings or sensations arise (are "triggered") when the person is exposed to the feared object/situation – or, in the case of addiction, to the substance, object or activity that they most intensely crave. As mentioned above, this application of mindfulness methods greatly facilitates the desensitization process.

MINDFULNESS METHODS AND DESENSITIZATION

Unified Mindfulness techniques – like those that you learned in Part One of this book – can be used to support the desensitization of "triggered" thoughts, emotions and physical sensations. **This is the heart of the UMED Process.**

Mindfulness methods provide surgical precision in the desensitization process – allowing it to unfold with greatest speed and efficiency. This is what makes the UMED Process so uniquely effective in supporting emotional repair.

Becoming mindfully aware of the strands of emotional reactivity associated with a specific trigger allows these strands to disentangle – and to be replaced with spacious, poised, even-minded equanimity. This facilitates the release of psychological suffering and supports mental–emotional wellbeing.

WHY WOULD ANYONE DO THIS?

At this point, you might legitimately be asking: *Why would I intentionally expose myself to something that I'm so afraid of that I've been strenuously avoiding it for months, years or decades? How does this make sense?!*

This is a common question, because facing our deepest fears can be scary. It takes courage and may require some hard work – a bit of fortitude and good old-fashioned elbow-grease. On the other hand, once you take the first step, it might end up being a lot easier than you imagined it would be.

And there are very good reasons to embark upon this journey. You can remind yourself of the reasons by contemplating and perhaps even writing down all the ways that fearfully avoiding an activity, situation, object or person prevents you from achieving your life-goals or simply enjoying comfortable, relaxed, anxiety-free time with friends or family. Imagine how your life would be improved if that worry, fear, anxiety or other emotional disturbance were dissolved. Exposure and desensitization protocols – like the UMED Process – can facilitate this kind of healing transformation.

It's not at all uncommon to feel some hesitation about intentionally exposing yourself to something you're afraid of. But here's an inspiring story that might provide some comfort and motivation.

CASE STUDY: THE CAT

I had a client who was experiencing intense sadness, anguish, anger and guilt around the recent death of her cat. She had taken her cat to the vet for a routine teeth cleaning procedure, which ended up including a tooth extraction.

In the days that followed, the cat showed signs of having an infection. My client repeatedly phoned the vet to ask if some other treatment was required to help resolve the infection, but the vet insisted that everything was fine. My client's gut feeling was that it was not okay – that her cat's health was declining in dangerous ways – but she decided to take the advice of the vet and do nothing. A few days later her cat died.

When this woman arrived in my office, she was grieving the death of her feline friend, consumed with anger at the vet and feeling immensely guilty that she hadn't followed her own instincts.

In that very first session I suggested that we employ the UMED Process, including an exposure and desensitization sequence. She felt hesitant and decided against it, because she was afraid that intentionally exposing herself to all the thoughts, feelings and images comprising this challenging situation would just make it worse, not better.

After several more sessions – and some gentle convincing on my part – she decided to give it a try. The trigger she used was a photo of her cat. She looked at this photo to trigger the emotional reaction – all the thoughts, feelings and internal images associated with the death of her beloved cat. This was the "exposure" part of the UMED Process.

She then applied a Unified Mindfulness method to these thoughts, images and feelings – until the level of intensity of her emotional disturbance had noticeably decreased. This was the "desensitization" part of the UMED Process. Since the disturbance level was not yet zero, she repeated this process a second time. The disturbance level decreased even more, though still wasn't zero – but at that point it was almost time to end the session. (Additional details about this process will be offered throughout the following chapters.)

The negative belief that this client uncovered was: *"I did not act quickly enough to save my cat's life."* And the empowering statement that she created to replace this negative belief was: *"I did the best I could under the circumstances. I will stop blaming myself."* While gazing at the photo of her cat, she repeated this empowering statement several times until it felt completely true.

At our next session, I asked this client how she was doing. She responded by saying that she had experienced a huge breakthrough in relation to her cat's death – and that she now felt great and had had an excellent week. This surprised me, given the extreme level of emotional anguish she previously had been suffering from. But her transformation and healing were genuine and just as complete as she reported. While typically it takes longer to achieve such dramatic results, every now and again the UMED Process, with exposure and desensitization, can and does work this quickly.

IS EXPOSURE THERAPY RIGHT FOR YOU?

How do you know if exposure and desensitization – as I employ it within the UMED Process – is something that may be helpful for you? It's likely to be useful if:

- You know exactly what triggers your worry, fear, panic or anxiety. In other words, you can identify the object, event, person or situation that most scares you.
- There is something important to you that you consistently avoid doing because of the worry, fear, anxiety or other disturbing thoughts or emotions that you experience.
- You sometimes try to stay safe, protect or hide yourself in ways that prevent you from living the life you most want to live.

If one or more of these statements is true for you, then an exposure and desensitization process is likely to be helpful for releasing the fear (or other disturbing emotions) and supporting a more satisfying engagement with your life. And I would enthusiastically encourage you to explore the UMED Process, which I introduce in detail in the following chapter.

THE PHYSIOLOGY OF
FEAR AND ANXIETY

Now, we're going to take a brief detour into the realm of human physiology – in particular, the physiology of fear and anxiety. The main attraction on this detour will be the amygdala: a small but powerful part of the brain. The amygdala is a major processing centre for emotions and directly influences the sympathetic nervous system, the fight-flight-freeze reaction to perceived danger.

THE MIGHTY AMYGDALA

The amygdala is an almond-shaped structure of cells nestled in the middle of the brain. It's part of the limbic system whose primary function is to process and regulate emotion and memory. The limbic system is composed of four main parts: the hypothalamus, the amygdala, the thalamus and the hippocampus. Here we'll be concerned primarily with the amygdala and secondarily with the thalamus and the hippocampus for their roles in the physiology of fear and anxiety.

Like the limbic system in its entirety, the amygdala plays a key role in processing and regulating emotions, particularly feelings of fear and anxiety. The amygdala is also involved in the creation of memories associated with emotional responses – it assigns emotional meaning to our memories. It also plays a role in decision-making and reward processing.

So, how is this tiny structure in the centre of your brain – the amygdala – related to feelings of fear and anxiety?

When we perceive something as a potential threat to our safety, the thalamus sends sensory information to the amygdala, which triggers a physiological fear response. The amygdala then activates the sympathetic nervous system, initiating a fight-flight-freeze reaction within the body. It also signals the hippocampus to store memories of the fearful event so we can avoid similar threats in the future, hence increasing our chances for physical safety and survival.

THE AMYGDALA'S ROLE IN DESENSITIZATION

In this way, the amygdala functions as our body's anxiety alarm. When it is triggered, a fight-flight-freeze reaction ensues. We go on high alert to respond to a perceived threat to our safety. When the amygdala's anxiety alarm becomes more and more sensitive to a particular trigger, this is known as **sensitization**.

On the other hand, when we feel more relaxed in relation to a particular situation, this corresponds to the amygdala – the anxiety centre of the brain – becoming less sensitive to a certain trigger. This is the physiological component of **desensitization**, the second part of any "exposure and desensitization" process.

When the amygdala learns through experience (for example, via exposure therapy) that something is not dangerous, this facilitates desensitization. Since the amygdala is designed to protect our body (this is its job) it may need a lot of convincing to be willing to turn down the anxiety alarm. For this reason, repeated exposure to the feared object, event, activity or situation is often required to complete the desensitization process.

Eventually, our anxiety "radar" may detect the trigger, but our amygdala "alarm" will not react to it like it did before. This signals a successful exposure and desensitization process – with the corresponding reprogramming of the amygdala.

GUIDELINES FOR SUCCESSFUL EXPOSURE AND DESENSITIZATION

If you've decided that an exposure and desensitization process might be useful, you may now be wondering: what's the best way to do this? What are the keys to successfully releasing fear/anxiety and other disturbing thoughts or emotions with the help of this technique?

These are great questions! And here are some general guidelines to enhance the effectiveness of this aspect of the

UMED Process. Each of these recommendations becomes even more accessible and easy to apply in light of the concentration, clarity and equanimity that you have already cultivated through your mindfulness practice (via the methods learned in Part One).

There are certain key elements of the exposure and desensitization process that are important to understand in order for it to be completely successful. These include:

1. **The process is prolonged, so we stay with it.**
   It's important to stay with the anxiety-producing situation that has been intentionally triggered until the fearful thoughts, images and feelings at least partially (and perhaps completely) subside. This is a key to starting to feel better. In each healing session, do your best to stay in the "exposed" situation long enough (while employing a Unified Mindfulness method); and do this often enough that you eventually become indifferent to or even bored with the trigger, as your level of equanimity increases.

2. **The process is repetitive, so we commit to the practice.**
   Repetition is important in learning any new skill and retraining our fear-response is no different. Remember our friend, the amygdala? Convincing this part of the brain that a specific trigger is not an *actual* threat to our safety can take time. That said, some people notice that their anxiety or other disturbing emotions decrease very quickly after beginning the exposure and desensitization process. And this may be true for you. But most people find that it takes consistent daily (or at least semi-weekly) practice to sufficiently retrain the mind and brain to restore a genuine sense of comfort and ease.

3. **We consciously focus on the fearful thoughts, images and sensations.**

   In an exposure and desensitization process, we are encouraged to focus on the feelings (the anxiety "alarm") that come up within the anxiety provoking situation. Why is this important? Because we are trying to convince the amygdala that this specific trigger is not actually dangerous. If we avoid these unpleasant feelings, we send the message that the trigger is, in fact, dangerous – and the time spent in the exposure session will not be effective.

   And this is where your Unified Mindfulness training – the methods you learned in Chapters 4–8 – becomes a huge advantage! You now have tools to help you become mindfully aware of (remain gently focused upon) the thoughts, feelings and images associated with the anxiety-producing situation. You can do this *directly* with the Focus In and Focus on Everything techniques, or *indirectly* with the Focus Out and Focus on Rest techniques. (See overleaf for tips on choosing a mindfulness method.)

4. **We do our best not to derail into safety/avoidance behaviours.**

   Safety behaviours include forms of distraction or avoidance that we may habitually use to protect ourselves from the perceived danger that our anxiety (with assistance from the amygdala) has convinced us is an actual threat. If you spend your exposure and desensitization session engaging in these avoidance behaviours, trying to protect yourself from the trigger – if you do everything in your power to avoid being exposed to the anxiety-producing situation – then the process is not going to work. These sorts of safety/avoidance behaviours will sabotage your exposure practice and the desensitization (via the acquisition of equanimity) that allows for healing simply will not happen.

Instead, be prepared for some discomfort and stay consistent with the practice. Have courage and fortitude! You're going to learn to "ride the wave" of fearful thoughts, images and sensations, remembering that while anxiety may be uncomfortable, it's not dangerous.

TIPS FOR CHOOSING A TRIGGER

A trigger is a mental image, situation or experience that activates the challenging emotional disturbance. In other words, a trigger is something that exposes you to all the thoughts, feelings and images associated with your specific psychological challenge.

For a person who is afraid of snakes, their triggers may include the *thought* of a snake, a *video* or *photograph* of a snake or a *rustling sound* outside in the bushes. In the presence of the trigger, the emotional disturbance is activated. If there are a variety of different triggers and you're not sure which one to use to begin the exposure and desensitization process, here are some tips for choosing one. Ask yourself:

1. Which trigger interferes with my life the most?
2. Which trigger – if fully desensitized – would result in the greatest improvement in my quality of life?
3. Does one trigger seem more "doable" than others? Would one be easier to start with, so I can at least begin to get my life back on track?

It's important to choose a situation and trigger that you feel confident you'll be able to work with to complete the exposure exercise. In other words, don't choose anything too overwhelming to start with. Remember that you can gradually increase the challenge, as you become comfortable and gain confidence in the process and experience some success with it.

HOW TO CHOOSE A MINDFULNESS TECHNIQUE

The Unified Mindfulness techniques that are most appropriate for the exposure and desensitization process are: Focus In, Focus Out, Focus on Everything and Focus on Rest.

Which of these four Unified Mindfulness techniques should you use? Each technique is powerful and can work well. That said, different people respond best to different mindfulness methods. Here are a few guidelines for making your own ideal choice:

• It's fine to follow your intuition. If a particular technique calls out to you, try it. (But a technique that at first seems most promising may turn out not to be.)
• Feel free to try different techniques and see what feels and works best. I always encourage mindful trial and error!
• If you find a technique that works, stick with it. But if it stops working or no longer works as well, try a different one.
• The technique that works best for you with one specific issue (or one particular trigger) may not be the one that works best with another.
• A technique that works beautifully for someone else who has the same issue may or may not work well for you.
• If at any point you feel overwhelmed, the Focus Out technique can be very helpful, especially if you speak the labels out loud. Focus Out can also be especially effective

in addressing anxiety, panic, flashbacks of traumatic events and compulsive urges.

- Consider whether you will do better by directly facing and engaging your suffering or by dealing with it more indirectly. To directly engage, try the Focus In or Focus on Everything technique; to indirectly engage, try Focus Out or Focus on Rest.

- Focus on Rest can be especially soothing, nourishing and comforting.

- Most importantly, never *aggressively* attempt by *force of will* to reduce or eliminate an emotional disturbance that has been triggered. Just practise the Unified Mindfulness technique and allow the disturbance to dissolve in its own time. *It is essential to engage in the exposure and desensitization process in this way to avoid a cycle of frustration in which you continue to suffer.* The key is to apply the mindfulness method with an attitude of welcoming, patience and benevolent indifference.

TIPS FOR IDENTIFYING
NEGATIVE BELIEFS

The cognitive behavioural component of the UMED Process includes identifying a negative belief that underlies the difficult mental–emotional situation that you're experiencing and replacing this negative belief with an empowering one.

Finding an empowering belief tends to be rather straightforward. The only essential guidelines are that it needs to be realistic and accepted as true. Within these parameters, you can let your intuition and creativity guide you in choosing one that calls to you – an empowering statement with which you authentically resonate.

But how does one go about identifying the negative or limiting belief that is fueling the psychological disturbance? This can be tricky as such beliefs are often subconscious and not immediately obvious.

In some cases, it may be as easy as asking: *When you think of the trigger image, what negative or limiting belief about yourself comes up?* You may get an answer to this question straightaway, which you can use to complete the UMED Process.

But what if such an answer is not forthcoming? What if you get stuck trying to find the negative belief underlying the anxiety-producing situation? Here are some tips and strategies for uncovering the negative belief:

1. **Become Mindfully Aware of Your Self-Talk**

   One of the best ways to uncover the negative belief associated with your psychological challenge is to pay close attention to your self-talk – to the content of your "inner voice." Very often, a stream of negative thoughts are the offspring of a particular negative/limiting core belief. So how this inner voice speaks to you can provide important clues to the negative belief that underlies it.

   Are there recurring themes in this mental chatter? Does your mind's inner narrative return, again and again, to certain topics – chewing on them like a dog gnawing on a meatless bone? Noticing these recurring patterns of negative thinking can help you identify the negative belief that's at the root of the mental–emotional disturbance you're seeking to resolve with the UMED Process.

   To assist in this process, you can write down any negative thoughts that you "catch" – and notice which ones come up repeatedly. Then ask yourself: what's the belief at the root of these thoughts? That is the negative/limiting belief at the root of your emotional disturbance.

2. **Use the Socratic Method of Dialogue**

   Another way to tease out the negative belief at the root of your mental–emotional challenge is to employ the Socratic Method of dialogue. This form of contemplative dialogue (among two or more people) is a common aspect of cognitive behavioural therapy. It features a series of focused yet open-ended questions that encourage honest self-reflection. The purpose of such contemplative dialogues is to uncover the deeper origins of more superficial thoughts, feelings or impulses. These are traced back to the underlying assumptions that have created them – like peeling away the layers of an onion.

   In the context of this kind of disciplined, thoughtful conversation with a trained therapist, you can explore your patterns of thinking, feeling and behaviour with genuine, relaxed and even playful curiosity. And this kind of dialogue can help you uncover the negative belief that's at the root of your specific mental–emotional challenge.

3. **Explore Themes of Helplessness, Worthlessness and Unlovability**

   Another strategy for identifying the negative belief at the root of your psychological disturbance is to focus on the themes of helplessness, unlovability and worthlessness, because negative and limiting beliefs are often an expression of these general categories.

   You might find that the negative belief at the root of your emotional disturbance is a variation on one of these common themes.

- Beliefs in the helplessness category are related to personal vulnerability, incompetence and inferiority. It could be something you believe you can't do; or an inability to act;

or a sense of being useless or ineffective; or something you feel you just can't handle.

- Unlovability-related limiting beliefs include the fear that you are not lovable or even likable; that you're incapable of intimacy; or that you are inherently stupid, ugly, awkward or undesirable.

- Worthlessness-themed negative beliefs include the belief that you are inherently unworthy; that you're insignificant; that your life is trivial or meaningless; that you're a burden to others; or the feeling that you've done something terribly wrong or unforgivable.

4. **Become Aware of Your Inner Rules**

   Another place to look for the negative belief at the root of your psychological challenge is within the realm of inner rules. These are assumptions about "how things are" that guide your behaviour.

   Inner rules are akin to a computer software program that runs in your mind and structures how you perceive and experience life. They are beliefs about what needs to happen for you to stay safe, or be successful or feel good, as you go about your activities in the world.

   These rules often orbit around themes of fairness or strategies for staying safe or getting ahead in the world. For example: "Good people don't gossip about others behind their back." Or "If you make one mistake, you're a bad person." Or "To avoid being disappointed, never try too hard at anything." Or "Avoiding conflict is the best way to stay safe."

   You may well discover the negative belief at the root of your emotional disturbance within this realm of inner rules.

5. **Consider Beliefs of Entitlement**

A final tip for identifying your negative belief is to consider beliefs of entitlement – the shadow-partner of unworthiness. While entitled beliefs may, on the surface, feel quite good – even empowering – at a deeper level they are just as limiting as beliefs rooted in a sense of unworthiness.

Believing that you're better than others, or that the world owes you something, or that others just don't understand you, or that you deserve special treatment, or that your needs are always more important than the needs of others are examples of beliefs rooted in the theme of entitlement.

Negative and limiting beliefs related to a specific issue are often rooted in a subconscious core belief that can be discovered using these tips/guidelines. Once you've identified the belief, you can begin to dissolve it using the UMED Process.

And now it's time for you to experience the process for yourself.

SUMMARY

- The UMED Process emerged out of clinical experimentation and an auspicious "accident" that resulted in the collaboration between exposure therapy and Unified Mindfulness.
- The exposure and desensitization process helps us to safely confront the objects, events, situations or people we are afraid of, in the context of a healing session. And, over time, these fears (and other disturbing emotions) can be successfully overcome.

- There are numerous tips and strategies that can support you with the various steps of the UMED Process: how to choose a trigger; how to discover the negative belief at the root of your disturbance; and how to choose a Unified Mindfulness method. (You can bookmark this chapter and refer to it when you need some guidance on effectively applying the UMED process.)

CHAPTER 10

THE UMED PROCESS –
SIX BASIC STEPS

WRITTEN WITH DONALD W MCCORMICK PHD

The Unified Mindfulness Exposure and Desensitization (UMED) Process is designed to facilitate emotional repair in deep and profoundly effective ways. It can help people heal from many challenging psychological conditions, such as anxiety, panic, addiction, obsessive-compulsive disorder, impulse control disorders and trauma. In this chapter, I'll be presenting the UMED Process in detail and offering step-by-step guidance on how to apply it to your own mental–emotional difficulties.

To begin, here are the six main steps of the UMED Process. Their definitions and detailed examples will follow:

1. Identify the issue.
2. Choose a trigger.
3. Identify a negative belief (usually about yourself) that is associated with the trigger.
4. Create an empowering statement that counters the negative belief and represents what you would like to believe about yourself that is true and realistic.
5. Apply the exposure and desensitization process, using a Unified Mindfulness technique, until the trigger no longer provokes an emotional disturbance.

6. Hold in your mind an empowering image or scenario related to how you would like to be, while you repeat the empowering statement until it feels completely true.

STEP 1: IDENTIFY THE ISSUE

The first step is identifying the specific mental, behavioural or emotional issue that concerns you. Being clear and precise about the situation to which you'll be applying the UMED Process is important. This allows the UMED "medicine" to be focused, and delivered to the proper location to do its healing work. Here are some examples of psychological issues that one might choose to address with the UMED Process:

- You are worried about your financial situation and cannot stop thinking about it.
- Your daughter has a serious chronic illness. Even though the chances of her dying from it are very small, you have a pervasive fear that the illness may kill her. As a result, much of the time you alternate between feeling agitated, angry and depressed.
- You are struggling with intrusive thoughts about physically hurting other people. You know that you would never actually carry out such impulses, but the thoughts continue to come into your mind.
- You are a 25-year-old woman who has been compulsively pulling hair out of your scalp for the past five years. You feel terrible about the bald spot on your head. You will not leave the house without wearing a hat to cover it up.
- You are a 28-year-old man who began having panic attacks after a bad ecstasy trip. You have great difficulty driving, because you fear you will have a panic attack behind the wheel.

- You are trying to study for your college entrance exams, but your obsessive worrying makes it difficult for you to focus.
- You are a combat veteran, and post-traumatic stress disorder (PTSD) symptoms are interfering with your ability to establish and maintain loving, supportive relationships.
- You've just lost your house in a forest fire. Your grief, panic and confusion feel overwhelming.

The UMED Process can work with issues that are mild and those that are extreme. It can work with emotional disturbances based upon reasonable concerns and ones that are entirely irrational. Its power to effectively deal with this wide breadth of issues lies in its combination of exposure and desensitization protocols with Unified Mindfulness methods, as described in detail in Chapter 9. Each of these, in and of itself, is powerful medicine. In combination, their therapeutic potency is enhanced exponentially.

Let's consider two hypothetical people: Wendy and Bruce.

WENDY

Wendy is a middle-aged woman who has a fear of snakes. It is especially bad at night. There's no particular reason for this fear; neither Wendy nor anyone she knows has ever been bitten by a snake. She lives on the third floor of a condo in the centre of Anchorage, Alaska – a state that has no poisonous snakes.

Nevertheless, Wendy is startled by any rustling noises she hears – particularly after dark. Any time she sees a coiled rope, cord or hose, she approaches it with great caution – or turns away. If she happens to see a video or a picture of snakes, she panics. For Wendy, even the thought of a snake causes hyperventilation, sweaty palms and a quickened pulse.

Wendy decides to use the UMED Process. She starts by identifying the issue she wants to work on and writes it down: *My crippling fear of snakes.*

BRUCE

Bruce is a 47-year-old hoarder who loves electronics equipment, computers and other tech gadgets. Several rooms in his large house are filled with such items, all of which he purchased on the internet. He never uses most of them.

Bruce's compulsion for internet shopping has gotten so out of hand that his wife of 20 years has threatened to divorce him. Bruce presently spends about $2,000 (£1,575) per month on internet purchases, which are eating up his retirement savings.

Bruce heard about the UMED Process after learning the Focus on Everything technique from Shinzen's Home Practice Program.* He decides that he wants to try the process.

Bruce starts by opening up Microsoft Word and typing in the issue he wants to work on: *Compulsively buying tech stuff on the internet.*

---

* The Home Practice Program (http://homepracticeprogram.com) is a program in which Shinzen Young and other United Mindfulness instructors use conference calls to teach United Mindfulness techniques to people around the world. Each conference call includes 50 to several hundred people. This allows the fees for the Home Practice Program to be kept very low.

Now it's time for *you* to identify a mental, behavioural or emotional issue that you would like to work on. Pick something that significantly reduces your wellbeing, such as an emotional response that is so painful that it interferes with your ability to function. (See the list at the beginning of this section for some good examples.) Avoid circumstances that are so traumatic that the assistance of a skilled therapist is necessary – for example, the emotional effects of having been sexually assaulted.

So, right now, put down this book and take a few minutes to choose the issue you'd like to focus on. You can write it down or just keep it in mind.

STEP 2: CHOOSE A TRIGGER

Your next step is to identify a mental image, situation or experience that activates the challenging emotional disturbance. This is called a "trigger" and will be a key element in the exposure and desensitization process because you'll use this trigger to intentionally "expose" yourself to the disturbing thoughts, feelings and/or images associated with the issue. A trigger can be something you see, hear, smell, taste or touch. It can be something you remember or visualize. It can be an event or situation. Choose a trigger that represents the worst part of the issue.

Often a trigger will create an emotional disturbance that is out of proportion to the actual threat. You may feel a strong impulse to run away, or to fight for your life or to freeze into silent immobility. Any of these reactions can interfere with your ability to deal with the situation in a genuinely skillful way. The UMED Process can relieve you of the disabling emotional reactivity associated with the trigger by employing Unified Mindfulness methods to disentangle the sensory strands that comprise that emotional reactivity.

Let's continue to follow Wendy and Bruce.

WENDY

Wendy writes a list of the things that trigger her fear of snakes. They are:

1. Hearing rustling noises (which triggers a startle response)
2. Seeing coiled objects (which triggers extreme caution or flight)
3. Seeing videos or images of snakes (which triggers panic)
4. Thinking about or imagining snakes (which also triggers panic)

She completes step two by choosing one of the triggers to work with. She chooses a video of snakes because it stimulates the most intense fear.

BRUCE

Bruce begins Step 2 by listing various triggers. They are:

1. Hearing about a new version of some tech gadget that he craves. An example of this would be hearing about the release of a new iPhone and feeling an uncontrollable urge to buy it.
2. Reading a review of some type of technology that he already owns (like a wireless speaker) in which the new item is rated higher than the one he owns (for example, the new speaker is given four stars and his only has three).
3. Seeing pictures of equipment and gadgets online, especially when the pictures are on websites that also sell them.

> Next, Bruce chooses the most damaging and powerful trigger of his urge to shop – seeing pictures of equipment and gadgets on online stores.

Now it's *your* turn to make a list of triggers that aggravate the issue you identified in step one.

Take out a piece of paper or create a new blank document on your computer. Make a list of the internal images, situations, sights, sounds, smells or tastes that might trigger unpleasant emotional responses in relation to your issue. Include any experience that automatically leads to unwanted fear, anxiety, anger, craving, sadness, despair, panic, worry, compulsive rituals, terror, hopelessness, or a strong urge to fight, flee or freeze.

When you're done, review your list. Then choose one of the items on the list that represents the worst part of the issue. Don't worry about choosing the right or best one, since you can always apply the UMED Process to other triggers later.

STEP 3: IDENTIFY THE NEGATIVE BELIEF ABOUT YOURSELF BEHIND THE ISSUE

In this step, you'll identify the negative belief about yourself that underlies the emotional disturbance associated with your issue. If you're feeling stuck or unclear about how to identity this negative belief, you can refer to the more detailed guidance provided in "Tips for Identifying Negative Beliefs" on pages 122–26. For examples of how this is done, let's return to Wendy and Bruce.

WENDY

Wendy asks herself: *What is the negative belief at the root of my fear of snakes?*

Her fear is largely irrational. It is not based on her actual experience. So, it takes Wendy some time to uncover the negative belief at the root of her fear. She needs to peel back her beliefs, layer by layer, like an onion.

She begins with the belief, *I am afraid of snakes because they are dangerous; they bite people and can kill them.* But that's not her actual underlying belief; it's common knowledge that snakes can be dangerous. She also knows that poisonous snakes don't live in Alaska, except in zoos or as exotic pets, so the chances of her actually encountering a dangerous snake are extremely small.

After a bit more digging in conversation with a mindfulness-centred therapist, Wendy gets to: *I've heard terrifying news reports of people dying from snakebites.* But those people don't live in Alaska, so Wendy keeps digging.

Finally, Wendy recalls an incident from her past. When she was a child, she watched a documentary about snakes. It was night and dark outside. The phone rang. She picked it up and was given the news that her brother had just been killed in a car accident. She thinks: *That's it! I associate snakes with darkness and my brother's death. So I'm afraid that snakes that appear at night bring shocking and painful death.*

Bingo: she has identified the core belief at the root of her suffering.

BRUCE

Bruce quickly identifies the negative belief that is behind his compulsive shopping issue. He chooses the negative belief: *I simply have to buy what I want when I go to websites that sell tech.* He chooses this belief because he feels out of control and he worries that he will never be able to break his shopping addiction.

Now it's time for *you* to identify the negative belief associated with your own situation. Ask yourself: *What is the core negative belief that leads to my emotional disturbance?*

Sit quietly for a few minutes, contemplating the question. Or write the question on a sheet of paper or in the document you created on your computer. Then write all the answers that come to you. Take as much time as you need for this. If you have trouble identifying your negative belief, it's fine to stop and return to the question an hour, a day or several days later. And, as mentioned above, you can always refer to the tips and strategies for identifying negative beliefs in the previous chapter for additional assistance.

Remember that a negative belief may be rational or irrational, understandable or not very understandable. It may even be downright weird. With the UMED Process, it doesn't matter which it is. What's important is that you do your best to identify the negative belief that's genuinely at the root of the issue. This may be easy or it may take work.

STEP 4: CREATE A REALISTIC EMPOWERING STATEMENT TO COUNTERACT THE NEGATIVE BELIEF

In Step 4, you find an empowering – and realistic – statement that counters the negative belief you identified in Step 3. This should be something that you would like to believe, even if you don't believe it now.

Here's how Wendy and Bruce complete this step.

WENDY

Wendy quickly settles on this realistic, empowering statement: *The chances of encountering a poisonous snake in Alaska are almost zero.* This is an objectively true statement and one that provides a direct antidote to Wendy's fear of a deadly snake biting her in her home state.

BRUCE

To counter his negative belief, Bruce crafts this empowering statement: *I can avoid buying anything from tech websites today by applying mindfulness to my compulsive urge.*

Bruce does not believe this at this time, because of the severity of his compulsive urges.

But he is already familiar with the benefits of mindfulness, and he wants to believe this about himself.

Now it's *your* turn to find an empowering statement that counters the negative belief at the root of your own issue. Remember that this statement needs to be realistic, not mere wishful thinking. It also needs to be one that you would *like* to believe about yourself. It should also provide a direct antidote to the negative belief. Within these parameters, you can let your intuition and creativity guide you in choosing one that calls to you – an empowering statement with which you authentically resonate.

So, with the negative belief that you identified in the previous step clearly in mind or written down in front of you, ask yourself: *What statement would be an effective antidote to this negative belief? What empowering belief would be its opposite and directly support what I'd like to believe about myself?*

Once you've come up with an appropriate empowering statement – one that you feel a clear internal *yes!* for – then write it down, because you'll need it for later steps in the UMED Process.

STEP 5: EXPOSURE AND DESENSITIZATION

This step is the heart of the UMED Process. In it, you *intentionally* trigger the emotional disturbance associated with your issue, assess the intensity level of this disturbance and then repeatedly apply a Unified Mindfulness technique to the thoughts, images and feelings that comprise the disturbance. For additional details on this exposure and desensitization process, please refer to my extended introduction in Chapter 9 (see page 103), which thoroughly addresses the most frequently asked questions about this process.

The exposure and desensitization process may feel uncomfortable at first – this is important to understand, so it doesn't take you by surprise. But stay with it, and you'll see for yourself that the discomfort will soon begin to diminish and, in most cases, eventually disappear.

This step is a bit complicated, so I've broken it into four parts.

Step 5A: Expose yourself to the trigger and rate your level of disturbance. In Step 2 you created a list of triggers that can activate the emotional disturbance. Now you're going to use one of these triggers to *intentionally* activate it.

You can use the trigger that you used in Step 2 or another one from your list. It's important to use a trigger that creates a strong reaction, but not an overwhelming one. Something that sends you running into the next room in fear would be counterproductive. You're likely familiar enough with your triggers to be able to discern which ones tend to provoke overwhelm and which ones set off more moderate responses. Choose one in the latter category.

Your trigger should also be something that's quickly and easily available. It could be a photo in your home, a video on the internet, a mental picture or a recorded sound; or it might be something you can touch, taste or smell.

Expose yourself to this trigger for as long as it takes to activate the suffering associated with your issue. Most triggers will do this quickly. You may only need a few seconds thinking of an image, watching a video, looking at a photograph or listening to a sound to activate fear, panic, craving or some other troubling emotion.

If the trigger that you've chosen doesn't activate this kind of strong response fairly quickly, then choose another one.

Once you've triggered the negative reaction, write down your rating of the intensity of the disturbance. You don't need to describe it; just rank the intensity on a scale of 0 to 10, with 0 being no disturbance at all and 10 being the highest level of intensity you can imagine.

As an example, let's use the issue of reducing the amount of sweet treats you eat. To expose yourself to your trigger, you might hold a doughnut up to your nose and smell it. You notice a strong craving to eat the doughnut. You give the craving a rating of 8.

Step 5B: Disengage from the trigger. Now, set your trigger aside, turn it off or walk away from it. Do whatever you have to do so that you're no longer exposed to it.

In the example with the doughnut, you disengage from the trigger by putting the doughnut in a place where you can't see or smell it. If your trigger is a photo or a video, put the photo out of sight or turn off the video. If your trigger is a mental picture – an image in your mind – then stop thinking about it and, if need be, intentionally think of something else.

Step 5C: Practise one of the Unified Mindfulness techniques (that you learned in Part One) for a few minutes. Then rate the intensity level of your disturbance again. Use one of the following four Unified Mindfulness techniques to skillfully welcome and engage with the thoughts, images and feelings that arise. While you practise your chosen Unified Mindfulness method, you are *not* trying to maintain awareness of your trigger. Simply practise the technique you have chosen for 2–3 minutes, staying with whatever arises.

- Focus Out (pages 71–72)
- Focus on Rest (pages 66–67)
- Focus In (page 74)
- Focus on Everything (aka See, Hear, Feel or Note Everything; pages 78–80).

After this round of practice, consider your level of disturbance (in this case, craving) once again. Write down your rating of its intensity, using the scale of 0 to 10.

Let's suppose that, after smelling the doughnut and rating your craving as 8, the mindfulness technique you decide to practise is Focus on Everything. You do it for 2–3 minutes. Then you examine your new level of craving and write it down. It's now 6. The intensity of your initial craving has now been reduced – from 8 to 6.

Step 5D: Practise your Unified Mindfulness technique and rate your disturbance level over and over again until your rating becomes 0. Then return to Step 5A.

Repeat Step 5C until your level of disturbance is 0. Then, return to Step 5A. For a second time, expose yourself to the trigger, and rate your disturbance level. Then go back to practicing your Unified Mindfulness technique and rating your disturbance level again and again (Step 5C) until it is 0.

So, with the doughnut craving example, you Focus on Everything for a few minutes, then rate your craving, then repeat, until your level of craving for the doughnut is 0.

Then you go back to Step 5A, expose yourself again to the trigger, and rate your craving. It is now 6.

So, you go back to Step 5C again and again until your craving level is 0.

Let's imagine that the third time you go back to Step 5A and attempt to trigger the craving by smelling the doughnut, the craving is down to level 5. So you go back to practising your mindfulness method for a few minutes and rate your craving again.

You keep repeating this process of exposing yourself to the trigger and rating your craving, then practising your mindfulness method and rating your level of craving again, over and over until Step 5A longer triggers any disturbances (or very little craving). Then you will be ready to move on to Step 6.

Another way to think about Step 5 is as two loops: the exposure loop and the mindfulness meditation loops.

The Exposure Loop. You expose yourself to the trigger and rate your disturbance. There are two ways out of this loop:

- If your response (disturbance level) is 0, you move on to Step 6.
- If it is larger than 0, you move on to the mindfulness meditation loop.

The Mindfulness Meditation Loop. You practise your Unified Mindfulness method for 2–3 minutes and then rate your level of emotional disturbance.

- If the disturbance level is greater than 0, you start the mindfulness meditation loop again – practising for a couple of minutes and then rating your level of emotional disturbance once more.
- You keep practising your mindfulness method followed by rating the intensity level of the emotional disturbance – until your disturbance level is 0.
- When your rating reaches 0, you go back to the exposure loop.

You may need to repeat this process of exposure and mindfulness meditation many times, over several sessions (taking days or even weeks) before you can go on to Step 6. This is fine – and quite common.

WENDY

For her trigger, Wendy chooses a YouTube video showing a pair of snakes. In the video, the snakes start out resting and then slither around slowly in their natural habitat in non-threatening ways. (She considered using another video, one showing an attacking rattlesnake, but decided that this would be too intense.)

(5A): Sitting comfortably, Wendy exposes herself to the trigger by starting the video. She immediately feels anxiety and agitation. She rates her disturbance level as 8.

(5B): Right away, she disengages from the trigger by turning off the video.

(5C): She immediately begins practising the Focus on Rest technique. She notes visual rest (darkness, light or a dark/light mixture behind her eyelids), physical rest (body relaxation), and auditory rest (internal or external silence), all using the labels *see rest*, *feel rest* or *hear rest*.

After a few minutes of practice, she evaluates her level of disturbance once again. It has decreased significantly – from 8 to 3. She writes down this new level of disturbance.

(5D): Wendy tries the Focus on Rest technique for a few more minutes. Then she evaluates her disturbance level again. She is dismayed to find that after a few minutes of meditation her disturbance level is back up to 8.

But she sticks with the Focus on Rest technique for a while longer. Over the next 10 minutes her disturbance decreases as she repeatedly practises Focus on Rest. Her disturbance level goes down to 3 but does not reach 0. Then she runs out of time and begins cooking supper.

(5A): The next day Wendy sits in front of her laptop for another session. She goes to YouTube and clicks on the same snake video. Her disturbance level is now 4, which is much lower than on the previous day.

(5B): She turns off the video and practises the Focus on Rest technique for a few minutes, then checks her disturbance level, which is now 0.

(5A): Because she reached a 0 disturbance level, she goes back to 5A and tries to trigger herself by playing the snake video again. To Wendy's surprise, she is unable to trigger a disturbance when she plays the video again. Suddenly, the video has lost its triggering power.

She watches the entire video from beginning to end – and feels no disturbance at all. She is now ready for Step 6.

BRUCE

(5A): Bruce sits down in front of his computer and exposes himself to a trigger by pulling up the Apple store website. There is a beautiful image of the latest iPhone, which just came out that day. He immediately feels tempted to buy it. As he gazes at the compelling photo, he rates his urge as 10.

(5B): Bruce immediately closes his eyes so that he is no longer exposed to the trigger. (He could also, if he chose, darken his screen.)

(5C): He starts practising Focus on Everything, noting his experience and labeling *see*, *hear* or *feel* with his eyes closed. He uses spoken labels for extra grounding, as well as a gentle voice to encourage equanimity. After 3 minutes, he notices that his urge level has lessened. He rates it as 5.

(5D): Bruce continues the Focus on Everything technique for a few more minutes. He notices that his urge has decreased and he rates the level as 3.

He repeats the mindfulness technique and then rating his phone-buying urge several times until his urge level is 0.

(5A): Bruce goes back to 5A – exposing himself to the trigger by looking at the image of the iPhone again. This time his urge level is lower than it was the first time he exposed himself to it. He rates the urge as 5.

(5B): Bruce closes his eyes to disengage from the trigger.

(5C): He uses the Focus on Everything technique for a couple of minutes and then rates his urge as 3.

(5D): He continues using the technique and rating his craving 4 more times, until his level of craving is 0.

(5A): Bruce opens his eyes and looks at the image of the new iPhone again. This time his urge level is 0. As he can no longer trigger an urge, he moves on to Step 6.

It's likely that you'll notice at least some improvement the very first time you go through the exposure and desensitization process. But that's not full desensitization, which means that you can no longer cause *any* disturbance with your chosen trigger but instead maintain consistent equanimity.

It's important that you monitor your progress by writing down your disturbance level each time you do each part of this step. And this means measuring how you feel both before and after each use of the Unified Mindfulness technique.

I also recommend comparing your results from day to day or week to week. If you like, make a chart to keep track of how you are doing over time. If that seems too detailed for you, simply take note of any changes every few days.

The **key to exposure and desensitization** is to **repeat the process** several times during each session and to **do multiple sessions** over a period of days – or, if necessary, weeks or months.

With practice, most people discover that their painful responses to triggers get weaker and weaker. This might happen in one session. It may take a handful of sessions. Or it might take 15, or 20 or 25. But the overall pattern is the same: the more times you use the desensitization and exposure process in Step 5, the less emotional suffering the trigger will likely engender.

Which of the four Unified Mindfulness techniques should you use? If you feel uncertain about which method would be best, refer to "How to Choose a Mindfulness Technique" on page 121 for some guidance. And remember, also, that it's fine to experiment – to try one technique for a while and then another to see which works best.

Friendly Cultivation: The Art of Mindfulness Gardening

What's most important is to never *aggressively* attempt, by *force of will*, to reduce or eliminate an emotional disturbance that has been triggered. Just practise the Unified Mindfulness technique and allow the disturbance to dissolve in its own time. *It is essential to engage in the exposure and desensitization process in this manner, in order to avoid a cycle of frustration in which you continue to suffer.* Once again, the key is to apply the mindfulness method – noting and labeling the various threads of sensory experience – with an attitude of welcoming and equanimity, with no demand or heavy expectation for how long the process is going to take. Think of yourself as a skilled gardener, planting seeds of mindful awareness. With proper care, they will sprout and grow. But you can't pull on the young sprouts to make them grow faster! Instead, be patient and trust that nature will take its proper course.

STEP 6: TRANSFORM YOUR BELIEF BY CREATING AN EMPOWERING MENTAL SCENARIO AND HOLDING IT IN YOUR MIND

In this step, you reinforce your empowering statement from Step 4 with an empowering scenario. And, if you like, you can amplify its power with a gentle smile. To begin, ask yourself, *"How would I like to be able to think, feel, speak or act?"* – and notice what feelings, words, phrases or internal images arise. Using these you can begin to weave an empowering scenario.

As you'll see, this is a slightly expanded version of Nurture the Positive and Self-Imaging – the techniques you learned in Chapters 7 and 8.

The first part of Step 6 involves creating a pleasant, realistic scenario – one in which you feel good and act in a positive, psychologically healthy way. Some examples:

- You are diabetic and are attempting to eliminate sweet treats from your diet. So, you might create an empowering image of being pressured to eat chocolate cake at a family dinner, but politely and firmly saying, "No, thank you," and fully enjoying an apple for dessert instead.

- You're feeling so sad and fearful about your daughter's chronic illness that your emotions interfere with your ability to care for her – or to simply enjoy her company. So, you create an image of you caring for her with equanimity and confidence, even in moments when she is in pain. You might also imagine the two of you enjoying a walk together, sharing laughter and happiness in spite of her illness.

- You're feeling so agitated as you study for an important exam that it's hard to concentrate on the material. So, you imagine yourself being calmly focused and relaxed as you study.

This empowering scenario should *primarily* relate to your *own* behaviour or your mental and emotional state, *not* to unrealistic external circumstances or events. For example, don't imagine your chronically ill daughter as perfectly healthy or envision yourself being able to eat a whole chocolate cake without it affecting your blood sugar levels. This step is not about wishful or magical thinking. It's about realistically addressing your suffering by developing positive mental and emotional responses to your circumstances.

In Step 6, you build upon the exercise completed in Step 4. But now, each time you repeat your empowering statement (*I'm not going to eat sweet treats today because they raise my blood sugar and aggravate my diabetes*), you *also* call up your imagined empowering scenario (turning down the offer of a slice of chocolate cake). You mentally hold that scenario for the entire time that you repeat your empowering statement.

After you hold (in your "mind's eye") your empowering scenario for 1–2 minutes, ask yourself how true your empowering statement feels. So, for example, *When I think of my empowering scenario* (turning down the offer of a slice of chocolate cake), *how true does my empowering statement* (I'm not going to eat sweet treats today because they raise my blood sugar and aggravate my diabetes) *feel on a scale from 0 to 10?*

As you call up the mental scenario, you may also gently smile – and enjoy the pleasant emotional and physical feelings associated with the smile. If the pleasure of the smile spreads to other places in your body, notice that as well. (Add the gentle smile only if it feels right in that moment.)

Sometimes, as people combine Steps 4 and 6 (integrating the empowering statement with the empowering image/scenario), they find themselves triggered again. If this happens, simply return to Step 5 and practise the mindfulness technique until your level of disturbance drops back to 0. Then, return once again to engaging with your empowering statement and scenario.

WENDY

The empowering scenario Wendy chooses involves a small garter snake. She imagines herself picking it up and holding it in her hands – with calmness, curiosity and pleasure. After holding it for a while, she puts it back in the grass and watches as it slithers away.

As she repeats her empowering statement (*The chances of encountering a poisonous snake in Alaska are almost zero*) and mentally holds this brief, empowering sequence of events, Wendy smiles gently – and enjoys the pleasant feelings that come up. She continues to imagine the empowering scenario while she repeats her empowering statement, until the felt truth of the statement is 10. She reinforces the felt truth of the empowering statement by repeating it several more times.

BRUCE

Bruce chooses a mental scenario in which he has lost interest in purchasing the new iPhone and instead has become interested in cleaning out one of the cluttered rooms in his house.

He imagines the empowering scenario as he repeats his empowering statement (*I can avoid buying anything from tech websites today by applying mindfulness to my compulsive urge*) and smiles for a few minutes. He then rates the felt truth of the statement as 8.

Bruce holds the empowering scenario in his mind again, while repeating the empowering statement for a few more minutes. Then he rates the felt truth of his statement as 10.

Now that he has reached 10, he repeats the process three more times – each time checking the truth of his positive belief, while holding the empowering scenario. Each time it is still 10.

Bruce writes his empowering statement on an index card and puts it beside his computer, so he will see it whenever he goes online. He memorizes the statement and, from then on, repeats it aloud three times a day. He also enjoys imagining his empowering scenario at the same time that he repeats his empowering statement at the end of his meditation each morning.

It is important to realize that this six-step process may take time, and progress is not always steady or linear. Improvement can be gradual or swift. Your desensitization may slow down, reach a plateau or even temporarily worsen. Eventually, though, the disturbance will largely or completely dissolve and the empowering belief will feel true.

WHAT TO DO IF YOU REACH A PLATEAU

If you reach a plateau when you use these techniques, continue doing what you've been doing. Some unseen momentum may soon propel you to a new level of healing.

If your disturbance does get worse instead of better or if you stay at a plateau for a dozen or more sessions, try one (or more) of the following:

- Use a different Unified Mindfulness technique. Choose from among the four suggested: (1) Focus Out, (2) Focus on Rest, (3) Focus In, or (4) Focus on Everything.
- Change your trigger to one that is less intense.
- If neither of the above provides relief and you simply can't desensitize, skip Step 5 and go straight to Step 6, where you focus on the positive. This works for some people.

Remember that the steps can be *repeated several times* during a single session – and that the process may require *multiple sessions* over a period of weeks or even months to be fully effective. I generally recommend one or two 15–20-minute sessions a day, every day. Of course, adjust this to suit your own situation.

TWO ONGOING SUPPORTIVE PRACTICES

I strongly recommend these two practices to support your healing and transformation after you have completed the six steps. They will help maintain, deepen, stabilize and refine the beneficial changes you've made using the UMED Process.

The first is to do your best to be mindful of your emotional reactions throughout your day. Become genuinely curious (without falling into harsh judgment or self-denigration) about how you respond emotionally in various situations. Just notice what kind of "software" seems to be running – what kind of programmed tendencies. Over time, this will help you gain a better understanding of yourself at the emotional and psychological level.

The second is to practise mindfulness whenever you feel any unpleasant emotional reactions. When such a reaction arises, simply turn your attention inward; note the presence of the reaction; and then apply a Unified Mindfulness method until you are no longer disturbed by the reaction or the reaction dissolves.

If you are in a situation that is too complex to allow you to use a fully fledged Unified Mindfulness method, keep doing what you're doing, but also be aware of *just seeing, just hearing* or *just feeling*. For example, if you're engaged in a heated discussion, you might maintain mindful awareness of your emotional body sensations. This means you still pay attention to what's going on in the discussion, but you keep part of your attention on body sensations associated with emotions. You might notice, say, a clenching of your jaw, a tightness in your chest or a knotted feeling in your belly, which are associated with your feelings of frustration and anger toward the person you're speaking with. Become mindfully aware of these emotional body sensations, giving them lots of space and relaxing into them.

Remember, this process *never* involves trying to repress, push away or eliminate any unpleasant experience. Instead, it involves mindfully noting and labeling that experience, allowing it to arise and stay for a time and then letting it dissolve on its own – allowing nature to take its course.

MAKE MINDFULNESS PRACTICE A REGULAR PART OF YOUR LIFE

Going forward, I recommend that you regularly practise one or more Unified Mindfulness methods spontaneously – whenever an issue arises for you or whenever else you like. For example, you might practise Focus on Rest, Focus In, Focus Out, Focus on Everything or any of the other techniques you've learned.

In addition to practising these techniques spontaneously, I also strongly encourage you to practise one or more of them regularly – on its own and more formally, rather than only in response to a particular issue. This will support you in becoming more mindful throughout your day.

I suggest at least 15–20 minutes of mindfulness practice a day, preferably seated on a cushion or a chair, with your spine in its naturally upright position. Alternatively, you can also do it lying down on a couch, bed or the floor if a seated position isn't possible for you. Devoting 30–45 minutes a day to your Unified Mindfulness practice is ideal.

As a bonus to yourself – a nourishing treat – after each period of mindfulness practice, recall a positive image of any kind. Then smile and feel the pleasure of the smile move through you.

These mindfulness methods, practised regularly, will help you to maintain present-moment awareness in your life. You'll experience for yourself how mindfulness enhances concentration, sensory clarity and equanimity. As a result, you'll be happier, you will understand yourself more clearly, you will experience less unpleasantness and will be generally more effective throughout your life.

KEEP REPEATING YOUR EMPOWERING STATEMENT

Another way to support your healing and transformation is by continuing to repeat your empowering statement (from Step 4) and *feeling* it as *true* at least three times a day (the more, the better). Keep doing this for as long as you feel it is needed. This may continue for weeks, months or even years. You are the best judge of this. For an added benefit, hold the empowering scenario (from Step 6) in your mind as you repeat your statement.

Now that you've experienced for yourself the six steps of the UMED Process, it's time to see how this uniquely powerful collaboration between exposure therapy and mindfulness can help resolve some specific psychological problems. The first one we'll consider, in the next chapter, is anxiety.

SUMMARY

- UMED stands for Unified Mindfulness Exposure and Desensitization. The UMED Process applies the principles and practices of Unified Mindfulness – in combination with exposure and desensitization tools and cognitive behavioural techniques – to issues that create mental or emotional suffering for individuals.
- You can use the UMED Process to address any issues that cause you mental or emotional disturbance – whether the suffering they cause is mild or extreme. It can work with emotional disturbances based on reasonable concerns and those that are wholly irrational.

- Practising mindfulness in action – being present with all activities and being open to whatever arises within you – will deepen your concentration, clarity and equanimity.
- Every moment of mindful awareness will help decrease your suffering and elevate fulfillment in your life.

CHAPTER 11

TAKING THE EDGE
OFF ANXIETY

In this chapter and the ones that follow, I'll show you some real-life examples of how Unified Mindfulness techniques and the UMED Process have helped people resolve their mental and emotional disturbances. These scenarios – which are based upon cases from my own mindfulness-centred psychotherapy practice – were chosen to demonstrate the efficacy of the UMED Process across a range of common psychological conditions: anxiety, panic, addiction, impulse control disorders and trauma.

This doesn't mean that these are the *only* mental health challenges that the UMED Process can successfully address. On the contrary, the UMED Process can be applied to a much wider range of issues. Even obsessive-compulsive disorder (OCD) or severe depression – which may not find a final cure – are excellent candidates for the UMED Process. Why? Because the UMED Process can help reduce symptoms and increase a person's coping ability by giving them tools to avoid getting caught up in and overwhelmed by thoughts and emotions, and instead maintain their equanimity even in the face of challenging circumstances. In this way, the UMED Process can vastly improve a person's quality of life – their capacity to function effectively in their daily lives – and enhance their overall wellbeing, even if the psychological condition isn't fully resolved.

The only psychological condition that the UMED Process is *not* appropriate for is schizophrenia and other psychotic or dissociative identity disorders. For someone who is deeply out of touch with conventional reality – experiencing hallucinations, delusions, disorganized thinking and/or distorted speech – the UMED Process is not the best choice for the first line of treatment. Such a person will likely require medication and should certainly be receiving care from a psychiatrist. In such cases, once this first line of treatment is in place, there may be an opportunity to incorporate Unified Mindfulness methods but only with continued psychiatric oversight. (An example of this kind of collaboration was presented in Shinzen Young's case study in Chapter 2, page 40).

However, the great majority of mental health challenges are not psychotic disorders – and so *can* be successfully addressed with the UMED Process. In this chapter, we'll begin with anxiety, a relatively common psychological disturbance.

We've all experienced occasional anxiety. In fact, feeling anxious, *for relatively short periods of time*, can actually serve a useful purpose. For example, it can alert us to genuine danger and energize us to create an effective response.

If you're canoeing down a fast-moving river and about to enter a narrow, rocky section of rapids, then feeling anxious is natural and appropriate. In fact, that anxiety will help you stay attentive and navigate safely through the rapids.

But when anxiety becomes chronic, habitual or extreme, it can do real damage to our mind–bodies. Chronic anxiety can also have debilitating effects on our relationships, our careers, our families and many other aspects of our lives. If you (or a loved one) is suffering from anxiety, the UMED Process can help you find relief from this condition and regain comfort and ease, as I will demonstrate in the following scenarios.

ANXIETY SCENARIO #1: SOMETHING BAD WILL HAPPEN TO MY PARENTS

Kevin is a ten-year-old boy who lives with his parents. He suffers from extreme anxiety and a fear that something really bad is going to happen to them while he is away at school. As an expression of this anxiety, he obsessively phones his parents on his Apple Watch – as often as ten times a day – to check up on them and make sure they're okay.

Kevin's parents feel frustrated by this anxious habit but they continue to answer all of his calls, which reinforces his behaviour.

Here's how Kevin, with the help of a trained UMED therapist, applies the six steps of the UMED Process to his situation. As part of the therapeutic intervention, Kevin's parents must gradually cut down how many calls per day they will answer. They gradually decrease it from ten calls per day to not answering any of the calls. Kevin is involved in this process.

Step 1: Identify the Issue Kevin's primary issue is the fear that something bad will happen to his parents while he is at school.

Step 2: Choose a Trigger The trigger that Kevin chooses to work with is an internal image of the police arriving at his home, letting him know that his parents have been in a car crash.

Step 3: Identify the Negative Belief The core negative belief that Kevin identifies is *I will not be okay if my parents are not okay*, which lies at the root of the anxiety.

Step 4: Create a Realistic Empowering Statement The empowering statement that Kevin and his therapist come up with is: *Even if my parents are not okay, I'm strong enough to be okay.* This empowering statement affirms that, even if one or both of his parents were injured or became ill, he would have the internal and external resources to navigate the challenge.

Step 5: Apply the Exposure and Desensitization Process
In this step Kevin applies the trigger that he has chosen to use – he imagines the police coming to his door with news that his parents had been in a car crash.

After clearly imagining this situation for a few seconds, Kevin rates his level of disturbance as 9.

Next, with the guidance of his therapist, Kevin applies the Focus Out technique to anchor him in external sights, sounds and body sensations. This technique indirectly supports the untangling of the mental and emotional disturbance.

After practising Focus Out for a few minutes, Kevin once again evaluates his level of disturbance. Now it is 5 – a big reduction.

Over the next two weeks, Kevin repeats the process of applying the trigger and then practising the Focus Out technique nine times on nine separate days. After the ninth day, the trigger no longer creates any disturbance for him at all. Although he still does not want his parents to be in a car crash, the thought of such a crash no longer creates psychological suffering or overwhelm for him.

Step 6: Create a Realistic Empowering Scenario Now Kevin is ready to further empower his healing process with an empowering image. The image that he chooses is of a police officer coming to his door to inform him that his parents have been in a car accident and he is handling it well, practising mindfulness with his reactions.

As Kevin holds in mind this empowering image, he repeats the empowering statement: *Even if my parents are not okay, I'm strong enough to be okay.*

Then Kevin pauses, and rates how true the statement feels to him. He rates it as 9.

After practising with this empowering image and his empowering internal message for five separate sessions, Kevin rates the truth of his statement as 10. He has successfully replaced the negative belief that was at the root of his anxiety with a realistic, empowering belief.

After nine sessions of the UMED Process, Kevin no longer experiences the anxiety that led him to repeatedly phone his parents from school and feels comfortable being away from them during school hours.

Be Mindful of Emotional Reactions on a Regular Basis From then on, as Kevin goes about his life, any time he notices unpleasant emotional reactions he applies the Focus Out technique until they decrease or dissolve.

As time goes on, he becomes more and more adept at noticing these reactions immediately and quickly applies the Focus Out technique instead of waiting for the emotional reactivity to become full-blown.

Make Unified Mindfulness a Regular Part of Your Life Kevin is not able to do Focus Out twice a day for 10 minutes. Instead, he finds himself naturally practising Focus Out whenever anxiety arises. He also creates and pins up a card in his bedroom with his empowering statement on it. He reads this statement, either out loud or to himself, at least three times a day, *feeling* it as *true*.

ANXIETY SCENARIO #2: WORK-RELATED FRUSTRATION AND ANXIETY

Michael is a 33-year-old emergency-room physician. Recently, Michael has been experiencing extreme anxiety and frustration in relation to his work. He finds it very difficult to work with other physicians who have differing opinions about how to perform their professional duties. Michael's anxiety is interwoven with deep self-doubt and it becomes so debilitating that he takes two weeks off from work to do intensive psychotherapy.

Step 1: Identify the Issue Michael wants to resolve his workplace anxiety, frustration and self-doubt.

Step 2: Choose a Trigger Over the course of his healing process, Michael works with four different triggers, in this order:

1. An image of him arriving at the door of the emergency room (ER).
2. An image of him walking from his parked car to the door of the ER.
3. A mini-scenario of him driving the last block to the hospital, then pulling into its parking lot.
4. A mini-scenario of him at home, getting ready for work – showering, getting dressed, having breakfast and then getting into his car.

Step 3: Identify the Negative Belief Michael discovers this belief at the root of his anxiety: *I'm afraid that I lack professional credibility.*

Step 4: Create a Realistic Empowering Statement Michael settles on this: *I'm a capable and credible physician and it's okay for others to have different opinions from me.* This directly counters his negative belief. It is also realistic because Michael has a good deal of advanced training and expertise, as well as an excellent track record as a physician.

Step 5: Apply the Exposure and Desensitization Process When he first begins this step, Michael vividly imagines himself arriving at the door of the ER. He holds this image for a few seconds until it triggers a disturbance in him. Michael rates this disturbance as 7.

Then Michael practises the Unified Mindfulness Focus Out technique for a few minutes. Afterwards, he rates his level of mental and emotional distress as 4.

Michael repeats the step, but this time does the Focus In technique for 10 minutes. Afterwards, to his surprise, his level of suffering has dropped to 0.

Step 6: Create a Realistic Empowering Scenario The positive image Michael creates is of himself debating (and perhaps even arguing) with another doctor about a medical procedure, *while feeling confident and credible.*

While holding this image in mind, Michael repeats aloud the empowering statement – *I'm a capable and credible physician and it's okay for others to have different opinions from me* – half a dozen times. At the same time, he smiles gently and enjoys the pleasant feelings that arise for him: comfort, warmth and spaciousness in his body, and ease and playfulness in his mind.

Michael then rates how true this positive belief feels to him. After his first time practising Step 6, the belief feels entirely true.

Michael immediately repeats Step 6 twice more in the same session. Both times, the positive belief continues to feel 100 per cent true to him.

After completing eight sessions of the UMED Process, Michael is pleased with his progress and comfortably returns to work.

Be Mindful of Emotional Reactions on a Regular Basis As Michael goes about his daily life, both at work and at home, he is mindful of any unpleasant emotional reactions that may arise. As needed, he applies a Unified Mindfulness technique.

Make Unified Mindfulness a Regular Part of Your Life
Michael enthusiastically adopts a formal practice of the Focus on Everything technique, which he practises every day at home for 10–15 minutes. When he has time, he does it for up to 45 minutes. Michael also creates an electronic file with his empowering statement written in large, colourful letters. He puts this empowering statement on all of his devices and makes it a point of reading it and repeating it to himself often.

ANXIETY SCENARIO #3:
WHITE COAT ANXIETY

Dina is a 40-year-old woman who has "white coat syndrome" or "white coat hypertension." People with this condition suffer from anxiety, heart palpitations and increased blood pressure when they are in a hospital or medical clinic or, in some cases, even in the presence of a medical device. Dina's white coat syndrome is especially triggered when she has her blood pressure taken.

Dina knows exactly how and when the problem began. Almost 18 years ago, when Dina ran her own successful code-writing company, she received an unexpected phone call from her lawyer. As the lawyer explained, Dina's own executive assistant, whom Dina thought was on vacation in Florida for two weeks, had embezzled nearly $80,000 from Dina's company. Dina received this call just a few minutes before going to her MD's office for her annual checkup. Cognitively, Dina is well aware that her white coat hypertension is not logical – but her symptoms and suffering persist nonetheless.

Most recently, Dina has become extremely anxious about her Bio-Electro-Magnetic Energy Regulator (BEMER) device – an expensive mat used to improve sleep and support the healing of other health problems. Although she spent thousands of dollars on her BEMER, she has become too terrified to actually use it. Whenever she lies on it, her heart begins beating so fast and hard that she fears she is having a heart attack.

Here's how Dina applies the six steps of the UMED Process to fully resolve her anxiety.

Step 1: Identify the Issue Dina's primary issues are the heart palpitations and anxiety she experiences when reclining on her BEMER or when having her blood pressure taken.

Step 2: Choose a Trigger Dina chooses to work with an image of receiving bad news via a phone call while she is wearing a blood pressure cuff.

Step 3: Identify the Negative Belief Dina discovers that the negative belief at the root of her issue is: *Medical devices will always trigger anxiety within me and I must get rid of the anxiety.* Dina wisely recognizes that she is not only anxious around medical devices but also anxious about that anxiety.

Step 4: Create a Realistic Empowering Statement Dina chooses this positive belief: *It's okay if anxiety arises for me when I'm around medical devices.* This positive belief skillfully addresses Dina's anxiety about her anxiety. This reflects an important aspect of mindfulness: not repressing or rejecting emotional responses but cultivating equanimity in relation to them.

Step 5: Apply the Exposure and Desensitization Process Dina imagines receiving a disturbing phone call while having a blood pressure cuff on her arm. She holds this image in her mind until it triggers strong anxiety. The first time Dina does Step 5, this takes only about 5 seconds – and she reports her disturbance level as 10.

Dina applies the Focus on Everything technique for 10 minutes, then notes her level of suffering. Now it is down to 4.

Dina repeats Step 5 twice more in two later sessions. After the second session her disturbance level has gone down to 0.

Step 6: Create a Realistic Empowering Scenario Dina imagines this mini-scenario: she is getting her blood pressure taken and she feels anxious at first, but accepts that anxiety with equanimity. She holds this image in her mind and at the same time repeats her positive belief – and smiles. After a few minutes, Dina pauses and asks herself: *How true does this positive belief feel?* She rates its felt truth as 10.

Be Mindful of Emotional Reactions on a Regular Basis From then on, as Dina goes about her life, she is mindful of emotional reactions if they arise. Then she applies the Focus on Everything technique until they decrease or dissolve.

After three sessions, Dina walks in the door of her therapist's office and immediately says, with a big smile, "I'm cured." She discusses how she is now able to use her BEMER with no problem at all and with a normal heartbeat. It is obvious that her work with the blood pressure anxiety also had a positive effect on the BEMER anxiety.

Make Unified Mindfulness a Regular Part of Your Life Dina commits to a formal practice of the Focus on Everything technique for 10–15 minutes twice a day. She also designs a wallet card with her empowering statement written on it and reads it aloud at least three times daily. She also repeats it from memory whenever she feels inspired to.

SUMMARY

- The UMED Process can be used to successfully resolve a wide range of psychological disturbances. The one exception is schizophrenia and other psychotic disorders, which require the care of a psychiatrist.
- The UMED Process can be used to successfully resolve or manage anxiety.
- The UMED Process can be enhanced by working with a *series* of trigger images, each one potentially more stressful or disturbing than the one before.

CHAPTER 12

TURNING PANIC INTO EASE

In this chapter, we'll explore scenarios involving panic attacks and discover how the UMED Process can support emotional repair for people suffering from similar conditions. Like anxiety, panic's primary emotional flavour is fear. Yet panic and anxiety are quite different.

Anxiety is typically defined as *excessive, persistent worry* about an upcoming event, whether significant or minor. Symptoms of anxiety include restlessness, hyper-vigilance, fatigue and irritability. Anxiety symptoms are often chronic.

Panic attacks are characterized by *short bursts of intense fear*, frequently accompanied by an increased heart rate, brief chest pain or shortness of breath. It's not uncommon for a panic attack to be mistaken for a heart attack, which is why someone experiencing a panic attack may rush to an emergency room.

Panic attacks generally last 30 minutes or less. They can be single events or occur repeatedly. Although many panic attacks are related to specific situations (an impending job interview, a late-night walk alone through a dicey neighborhood and so on), an episode of panic can also arise out of nowhere, unrelated to any stress or circumstance.

If you've been struggling with panic attacks or know someone who has, you can take comfort and hope in the fact that there are ways to unwind this condition and the UMED Process is one of them. In the scenarios presented here, you'll see how Unified

Mindfulness techniques and the UMED Process can help to resolve panic symptoms.

PANIC SCENARIO #1: PANIC IS GOING TO RUIN MY LIFE

Alison is a 48-year-old attorney. She has a panic disorder that's rooted in childhood trauma. She was recently hospitalized for several days because of severe panic attacks.

Step 1: Identify the Issue Alison's issues are clear and twofold: the severe panic attacks themselves and her fear that these attacks may ruin her life.

Step 2: Choose a Trigger Alison lists several triggers; after some deliberation, she chooses to work with an image of herself as a patient in a psychiatric hospital.

Step 3: Identify the Negative Belief Alison identifies this belief: *I will never be healed of panic and it will ruin my life.*

Step 4: Create a Realistic Empowering Statement Alison counters the negative belief with this empowering statement: *I'm safe. Even extreme emotional reactions can pass quickly when I practise a mindfulness technique.*

Step 5: Apply Exposure and Desensitization Process Alison imagines herself being in a psychiatric hospital. After only a few seconds, the panic sensations appear, then quickly worsen. Alison evaluates her level of disturbance as 10.

Alison applies the Focus Out technique to anchor her awareness in external sights, sounds and tactile sensations.

After practising this technique for a few minutes, she measures her level of disturbance again. It is now down to 4.

She repeats Step 5 again a few hours later – after which her disturbance level is down to 0.

Step 6: Create a Realistic Empowering Scenario Alison creates a mini-scenario of herself relating skillfully to feelings of panic by using a mindfulness practice. This creates a positive feedback loop – Alison practises mindfulness partly by imagining herself practising mindfulness.

As she holds this image in mind, she smiles gently and appreciates the pleasant emotional and physical sensations that arise. At the same time, she repeats her positive belief: *I'm safe. Even extreme emotional reactions can pass quickly when I practise a mindfulness technique.*

Alison rates how true this positive belief feels. After her first time doing Step 6, her rating is 9. After her second, it is 8. After her third, fourth and fifth – all done in the same session – it's 10.

So, Alison continues to practise.

Be Mindful of Emotional Reactions on a Regular Basis From then on, as Alison goes through her day, she watches for and notes any unpleasant emotional reactions that may arise within herself. When she notices them, she immediately applies a Unified Mindfulness technique for as long as it takes for those reactions to mostly or completely dissolve. Alison notices remarkable overall improvements in her life and accomplishes her goal of greater emotional stability.

Make Unified Mindfulness a Regular Part of Your Life Alison commits to a formal practice of the Focus Out technique for 15–20 minutes each day. She also writes her positive belief on a card, posts that card on her kitchen bulletin board and repeats the belief aloud several times daily, *feeling* it as *true*.

PANIC SCENARIO #2: PANIC ATTACKS WHILE DRIVING

Marilyn is a 50-year-old chiropractor. Two years ago, she was in a very serious car accident. Since then, she has experienced frequent panic attacks, both while driving and while riding in cars as a passenger. At times, she can barely drive to the neighbourhood grocery store or movie theatre without being overwhelmed by panic. On her way to her first therapy appointment, she has to pull over several times to cry and collect herself.

The primary component of Marilyn's healing is the Focus Out technique. She learns to apply this mindfulness technique as soon as she notices the slightest feeling of panic. She also learns to stay with the technique *throughout the entire attack*, until she once again feels balanced and at ease.

After her first 50-minute session using the Focus Out technique, Marilyn gets in her car and practises it. As she drives away, she realizes that her panic sensations have decreased by 60 per cent! After about a week of daily practice sessions, Marilyn finds that the panic attacks have become extremely infrequent. After five sessions, they have disappeared completely.

In Marilyn's case, the full UMED Process isn't necessary. Because she finds the Focus Out technique so effective, she is able to leapfrog some of the usual steps.

With her panic attacks fully resolved, Marilyn applies mindfulness techniques to other issues. Over time, she experiences inspiring positive changes across many aspects of her life. Ultimately, for Marilyn, the car accident is the catalyst for multiple streams of healing.

SUMMARY

- Sometimes a single Unified Mindfulness technique – rather than the full UMED Process – is all that's needed to unwind panic or other mental and emotional suffering.
- The Focus Out technique can be a particularly beneficial tool for healing panic attacks.

CHAPTER 13

DISSOLVING ADDICTIONS AND OTHER NEGATIVE BEHAVIOURS

Chances are that you or someone you know has been affected by addiction. Whether it's a diagnosed substance use disorder involving alcohol, nicotine, pharmaceuticals or illicit drugs – or an addiction to sugar, gambling, pornography, video gaming, shopping or mobile phone use – you've seen for yourself how addiction can undermine a person's physical, mental, emotional and social wellbeing, often in devastating ways. The good news is that the UMED Process can help unwind addictive behaviour and restore psychological balance.

Most addictions and negative behaviours begin in a very innocent way, with one or more of these desires:

- To feel good – to enjoy feelings of pleasure
- To get relief – to alleviate physical or emotional pain
- To do better – to enhance physical or mental performance
- To fit in – to be accepted, especially by peers
- To try something new – to follow a natural curiosity.

None of these motivations is necessarily a problem. The problem arises when the addictive substance or behaviour, which was originally a friendly guest, becomes a master and tormenter.

Addictions usually have a physiological component and they almost always involve mental and emotional dynamics.

Sometimes, genetics plays a role as well. At their root, addictions all arise out of a deep hunger for something that can never be fulfilled by *any* substance or activity.

Addiction can only be fully healed by connecting with our own innate wholeness. Other forms of healing may be needed as well, but this experience of wholeness is always essential.

In this book, I deliberately sidestep all debates about the physiological, psychological and spiritual components of addiction. Instead, in this chapter, I'll simply offer a few examples of how a skillful application of the UMED Process – and a related protocol – can help unwind addictive patterns.

As you'll see, this new protocol is very similar to what I've previously presented as the six-step UMED Process. However, there also are a few differences, which I have found to be very useful in helping people heal from addiction. This variation of the UMED Process that I use to resolve addictive behaviour is called the Release and Empowerment Protocol for Overcoming Negative Behaviours.

RELEASE AND EMPOWERMENT PROTOCOL FOR OVERCOMING NEGATIVE BEHAVIOURS

The Release and Empowerment Protocol consists of four phases and eight steps. While it might seem a bit complicated at first, there's an underlying simplicity that you'll come to appreciate. Like the UMED Process, there's an exposure and desensitization process that utilizes Unified Mindfulness techniques.

Where this new addiction protocol *differs* a bit from the basic UMED Process is in its **cognitive-behavioural component**. As you may recall, the cognitive component of the UMED Process includes identifying a negative belief that is at the root of the emotional disturbance, and then creating an empowering statement and visualized scenario that serves as an antidote to the negative belief.

The cognitive component of this Release and Empowerment Protocol includes (1) contemplating – through both visualization and story-telling – the *damaging consequences* of the negative behaviour (for example, the addiction or impulse control disorder); and then (2) contemplating – through both visualization and story-telling – the *beneficial consequences* of the behaviour change. Also, the empowering statement in the addiction protocol is crafted to counteract the negative *behaviour*, while in the basic UMED Process the empowering statement is created as an antidote to the negative *belief*.

So, is this Release and Empowerment Protocol appropriate only for addiction – for diagnosed substance use disorders – or are there other psychological conditions that it can also effectively be applied to? This protocol is appropriate for any type of negative behaviour that has clear worldly (social, interpersonal, work/career, financial and so on) consequences. This includes, for example, impulse control disorders such as compulsive hair-pulling (trichotillomania), compulsive skin-picking, chronic nail-biting, pyromania, intermittent explosive disorder, kleptomania, pathological gambling, compulsive shopping or compulsive sexual behaviour.

Now, let's explore in more detail the four phases and eight steps of this protocol, which, once again, is simply a variation of my basic UMED Process that is designed to facilitate the resolution of addictive behaviours even more efficiently.

THE FOUR PHASES OF THE RELEASE AND EMPOWERMENT PROTOCOL

In applying this protocol, you will pass through four main phases:

- **Phase I** (Step 1) is equivalent to the first two steps of the UMED Process – identifying your issue and choosing a trigger. In addition, you will prepare an empowering statement that's related to the negative behaviour you wish to transform. This is your "prep work" for the session.

- **Phase II** (Steps 2–4) corresponds to Step 5 of the UMED Process. Here you apply the exposure and desensitization process: you trigger the negative urge or craving and observe it with mindful awareness (in a state of high concentration, sensory clarity and equanimity) until the urge or craving weakens or perhaps completely dissolves.
- In **Phase III** (Steps 5 and 6), you contemplate the consequences that the negative behaviour has or could have in your life.
- In **Phase IV** (Steps 7 and 8), you contemplate the beneficial effects of the positive behaviour change.

Now, let's look more closely at each of the eight steps of this addiction protocol.

THE EIGHT STEPS OF THE RELEASE AND EMPOWERMENT PROTOCOL

The eight steps of the Release and Empowerment Protocol for Overcoming Negative Behaviours are as follows.

Step 1: Prepare a Trigger and Empowering Statement

Once you're clear on the specific addictive behaviour you wish to transform, then decide on a *trigger* that will bring about a significant urge or craving. The trigger could be a physical object such as a doughnut, an empty beer can, a cigarette, an internet photo and so on, or just something you imagine/visualize. Then, choose an empowering statement that will strongly motivate you to release the negative behaviour. A recommendation would be a statement that begins with,

"I'm not going to ... today because ...". For example: "I'm not going to drink alcohol today because I value my health, safety and personal dignity."

Step 2: Trigger the Urge or Craving This can be done by looking at something, smelling and holding or touching something. As mentioned above, mental images may also be used.

Step 3: Deconstruct the Urge or Craving Using a Unified Mindfulness Technique After you attempt to trigger the urge or craving, rate the urge or craving level on a scale of 0 to 10: 0 meaning that there is no urge or craving present and 10 indicating an urge or craving with the greatest possible intensity. Zero in this case is just another way of saying that you can't trigger an urge or craving. That's not a problem. If that happens, go immediately to Step 5. But if you are able to trigger the urge or craving, then begin practising a mindfulness technique from the Unified Mindfulness system. The Focus on Everything technique (see pages 78–80) works well for most people. Apply that technique to the urge or craving until the urge or craving level is 0.

Step 4: Try to Re-trigger the Urge or Craving Expose yourself to the trigger again and rate your urge or craving level. If there is still an urge or craving, repeat Step 3. When you can no longer trigger an urge or craving, move on to Step 5.

Step 5: Visualize the Negative Consequences of the Behaviour Visualize the negative consequences associated with the negative behaviour while repeating the empowering statement from Step 1 to yourself or out loud. Continue for around 1 minute and then check in with yourself to see how true the statement feels. Rate the felt truth of the statement on a scale of 0 to 10, 0 meaning that the statement feels completely false and 10 meaning that the statement feels completely true. Repeat the statement again for about 1 minute and check in with yourself. Ideally you want the statement to feel completely true or close to it for 3 minutes in a row before you move on to Step 6.

Step 6: Tell Yourself a Story about the Negative Consequences of the Behaviour Speak this story either out loud or internally to yourself. Devote around 1 minute to this part of the process. For example: "I ended up in the hospital after my last bout of drinking because I crashed the car and came close to being killed. It was a nightmarish experience." In Step 5 you *visualized* the negative consequences of the behaviour while repeating the empowering statement. In contrast, here you are creating a *verbal narrative* – a story that you speak out loud or to yourself.

Step 7: Visualize the Positive Consequences of the Behaviour Change Visualize the positive consequences of the behaviour change while repeating the empowering statement from Step 1 to yourself or out loud, for at least 1 minute. How would you like to be? Imagine your life as a person who has freed themselves from the negative behaviour. Then check in with yourself to see how true the statement feels. Rate the felt truth of the statement on a scale from 0 to 10, 0 meaning that the statement feels completely false and 10 meaning that the statement feels completely true. Repeat the statement for about 1 minute and check in with yourself again. Ideally you want the statement to feel completely true for 3 minutes in a row before you move on to Step 8.

Step 8: Tell Yourself a Story about the Positive Consequences of the Behaviour Change Tell a story to yourself – or speak it out loud – that highlights the positive consequences of changing the negative behaviour. Continue this narration for at least 1 minute. Include all the possible rewards and benefits of releasing the negative behaviour.

The Release and Empowerment Protocol for Overcoming Negative Behaviours

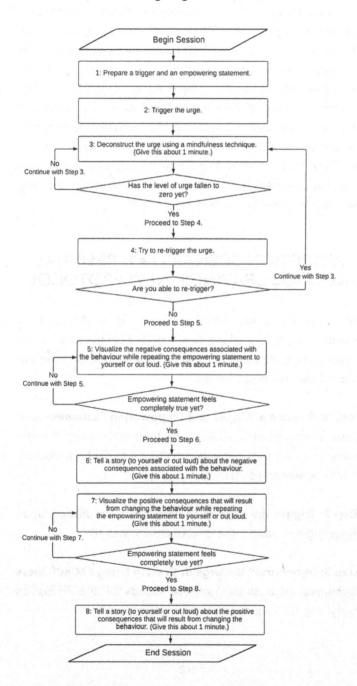

Begin Session

1: Prepare a trigger and an empowering statement.

2: Trigger the urge.

3: Deconstruct the urge using a mindfulness technique. (Give this about 1 minute.)

No
Continue with Step 3.

Has the level of urge fallen to zero yet?

Yes
Proceed to Step 4.

4: Try to re-trigger the urge.

Yes
Continue with Step 3.

Are you able to re-trigger?

No
Proceed to Step 5.

5: Visualize the negative consequences associated with the behaviour while repeating the empowering statement to yourself or out loud. (Give this about 1 minute.)

No
Continue with Step 5.

Empowering statement feels completely true yet?

Yes
Proceed to Step 6.

6: Tell a story (to yourself or out loud) about the negative consequences associated with the behaviour. (Give this about 1 minute.)

7: Visualize the positive consequences that will result from changing the behaviour while repeating the empowering statement to yourself or out loud. (Give this about 1 minute.)

No
Continue with Step 7.

Empowering statement feels completely true yet?

Yes
Proceed to Step 8.

8: Tell a story (to yourself or out loud) about the positive consequences that will result from changing the behaviour. (Give this about 1 minute.)

End Session

This flow-chart illustrates the various steps of the Release and Empowerment protocol, and how they are related to one another: The following case demonstrates a client making use of the Release and Empowerment Protocol previously described. Prior to my development of this most recent (and, in my experience, most effective) protocol, I employed a related but slightly different protocol to help people recover from addiction or impulse-control disorders. Although the cases that demonstrate the use of the older model were also marked by success (as you'll see below), I have found that the addition of the extra steps has made a significant difference in successfully releasing the negative behaviour patterns.

ADDICTION SCENARIO #1: RESIDUAL ALCOHOL CRAVINGS (NEW PROTOCOL)

Jake is a 47-year-old nurse employed by an Albuquerque hospital. He began drinking destructively from the time he was a young man. He reported that he recently quit drinking but was still experiencing cravings.

Step 1: Prepare a Trigger and Empowering Statement Jake chose an empty bottle of beer as his trigger. He chose, "I'm not going to drink today, because I don't want to die from alcohol" as his empowering statement.

Step 2: Trigger the Urge or Craving In the first session, upon triggering the craving, the level of craving was 10.

Step 3: Deconstruct the Urge or Craving Using a Mindfulness Technique After three 1-minute rounds of the Focus on Everything technique, Jake's craving level was 0.

Step 4: Try to Re-trigger the Urge When Jake tried to retrigger the craving, his level of craving was 5. He deconstructed the craving using Focus on Everything until the craving level was 0. When he tried to retrigger the craving the craving level was 0. He moved on to the next step.

Step 5: Visualize the Negative Consequences of the Behaviour Jake visualized many negative consequences of drinking including coming close to death in the hospital.

He held the visualization as he repeated his statement, "I'm not going to drink today because I don't want to die from alcohol." After doing this for 1 minute, the felt truth of the statement was 10. He did it for another minute and the felt truth of the statement was 10. He did this for a further minute and the felt truth of the statement was 10. He moved on to the next step.

Step 6: Tell Yourself a Story about the Negative Consequences of the Behaviour Jake told a story of the extremely negative experiences that had resulted from his drinking, as well as the potential for disaster in his life if he continued. He moved on to the next step.

Step 7: Visualize the Positive Consequences of the Behaviour Change Jake visualized a life of freedom from alcohol. He envisioned being able to accomplish his goal of becoming a physician. He imagined a more fulfilling relationship with his fiancée and his children. And he visualized these positive consequences while he repeated his empowering statement. He repeated the statement and held the visualization until the felt truth of the statement was 10 for 3 minutes in a row.

Step 8: Tell Yourself a Story about the Positive Consequences of the Behaviour Change Jake discussed his happiness and the freedom that he felt without alcohol in his life. He talked about the improvements in all aspects of his life, and especially his family relationships.

Summary: On the fifth therapy session, Jake could no longer trigger a craving and he could barely smell any alcohol from the empty beer bottle. On the sixth session, he could no longer trigger a craving. Since then, we have started the session by attempting to trigger the craving. Since no craving has been triggered, we have moved on to the other steps of the protocol to reinforce relapse prevention.

The remaining case studies employ the four main phases of the Release and Empowerment Protocol, but with some slight variations in the steps.

ADDICTION SCENARIO #2: ALCOHOLISM AND BINGE DRINKING (OLDER PROTOCOL)

Loretta is a 31-year-old woman who suffers from PTSD, social anxiety disorder, chronic alcoholism and she also binge drinks. Her binges often end in her blacking out. Loretta has tried several different forms of treatment, including a year of in-patient treatment, individual therapy and participation in the Mindfulness-Based Stress Reduction alcoholism study at the University of New Mexico. None of these have helped her heal from alcoholism and binge drinking.

Loretta's first step toward healing is to learn the Focus Out and Focus on Everything techniques. She practises these techniques regularly for about two months, addressing her PTSD issues in therapy, thus establishing a strong foundation of mindfulness. This enables her to address some of her other issues, which are related to social anxiety. Eventually she feels ready to apply the

UMED Process to her alcohol addiction. Here is how she works through the then-five steps of the addiction protocol.

Step 1: Identify the Issue and Choose an Empowering Statement Loretta's issue is alcoholism with binge drinking. She chooses as her empowering statement, "I'm not going to drink today because I don't want cirrhosis." This statement is designed to empower her and deter her from engaging in the addictive behaviour.

Step 2: Choose a Trigger Loretta's trigger is a small bottle of Jim Beam bourbon.

Step 3: Apply Exposure and Desensitization Loretta triggers her craving intentionally by smelling the alcohol from a small bottle of bourbon. After a few seconds her craving for alcohol is fully activated. Loretta rates the strength of the craving as 8.

Loretta chooses the Focus on Everything technique as a way to begin unwinding the strands of sensory experience that constitute the craving. She chooses to work with her emotional body sensations associated with the craving and labels these as *feel*. After a few minutes of practising this technique, she once again rates the strength of the craving, which has now dropped to 4. She continues until her craving level is 0. At that point she can no longer trigger a craving by smelling the alcohol. She moves on to Step 4.

Step 4: Choose a Mental Scenario that Represents the Worst Possible Consequences of the Addiction Loretta chooses an image of herself being hospitalized with cirrhosis of the liver. She holds the image in her mind as she repeats her empowering statement, "I'm not going to drink today, because I don't want cirrhosis." After repeating this empowering statement several times out loud and sometimes to herself while holding the image of the consequences, she asks herself as she smells the alcohol: *How true does this empowering statement feel to me?* She rates its felt truth as 7. Loretta repeats this process until the statement feels completely true (10) as she smells the alcohol and holds the consequential image. She then tells a story about the devastating consequences of her alcoholism. Then she moves on to Step 5.

Step 5: Hold an Empowering Image or Scenario in Your Mind (how you would like to be) Along with the Empowering Statement (I'm not going to drink today because ...) Loretta envisions a mini-scenario of herself having a good time with others who are drinking but in which *she turns down alcohol and drinks a bottle of sparkling apple juice.* She repeats this process until the statement feels completely true. Then she tells a story about the amazing rewards of being able to turn down alcohol and stay sober.

Within two weeks of working with her therapist in this way and doing sessions at home, she develops an aversion to alcohol. She cannot tolerate smelling it or thinking of it without feeling disgusted.

Be Mindful of Emotional Reactions on a Regular Basis Day by day in her life, Loretta makes it a point to apply the Focus on Everything technique to any unpleasant emotional sensations as soon as they arise. By addressing and transforming them immediately, she's able to dissolve them before they escalate into serious cravings for alcohol.

Make Unified Mindfulness a Regular Part of Your Life Loretta commits to a formal mindfulness practice of 20 minutes, twice per day: first thing in the morning and in the evening right before bed. She also puts her positive statement on the home screen of her computer and reads that statement out loud or to herself several times daily. While reading the positive statement and *feeling* it as *true*, she sometimes also brings to mind her positive image and enjoys the pleasure of a gentle smile.

A few months later, during a time of great emotional upheaval and distress, Loretta relapses and spends an evening drinking. However, the very next day, she once again applies the steps of the UMED Process and immediately resumes her alcohol-free lifestyle. She realizes that this is the first relapse she has ever had that did not lead to continued drinking. She then addresses the emotional issues leading to the relapse with her therapist.

Today, Loretta is free of cravings and has not taken a drink for almost two years. She tells people close to her that this is the first form of addiction treatment that has led to a complete release of a craving for alcohol.

ADDICTION SCENARIO #3: HEALING FROM A SUGAR ADDICTION (OLDER PROTOCOL)

Sean is 17 and doing poorly in school. He's unable to concentrate in the classroom. He was told that he might have ADD but he informs his therapist that he believes his real problem is sugar. He admits that he eats lots of sugar throughout the day. Although eating that much sugar makes him feel sick and his concentration very poor, Sean just can't stop.

Step 1: Identify the Issue and Choose an Empowering Statement Sean's issue is sugar addiction, which includes uncontrollable bingeing on anything chocolate. He chooses as his empowering statement, "I'm not going to eat chocolate today because I want to be able to concentrate and graduate from high school."

Step 2: Choose a Trigger Sean chooses an internet photo of chocolate as the trigger that he will work with first. (Later in his healing process, he uses actual chocolate to trigger the cravings.)

Step 3: Apply Exposure and Desensitization Sean looks at a photo of a decadent piece of chocolate until his craving is activated. He evaluates the intensity of the craving as 10. Then Sean applies the Focus on Everything technique to the strands of sensory experience comprising his cravings. After a few minutes of practice, he reevaluates the level of the craving. It has now gone down to 5. Sean continues the mindfulness technique until his craving is 0. He then attempts to trigger the craving by looking at the internet photo again. He evaluates his craving as 3. He goes back to the mindfulness technique until his craving is 0. He then attempts to trigger the craving again by viewing the internet photo but he can no longer trigger it … it's 0. He moves on to Step 4.

Step 4: Choose an Image that Represents the Worst Possible Consequences of the Addiction Sean chooses an image of himself not graduating from high school because of poor concentration resulting from his sugar addiction. He then holds the image in his mind as he repeats his empowering statement, "I'm not going to eat sugar today because I want to be able to concentrate and graduate from high school." He holds the image and repeats the statement over and over five times, until it feels totally true and he rates it as 10. He then tells a story about the consequences of his addiction. He now moves on to Step 5.

Step 5: Choose an Empowering Image and Hold it in Your Mind with the Empowering Statement Sean now chooses an empowering image. He imagines himself walking past the candy store on the way to school. Now he repeats his empowering statement in his mind as he holds the empowering image. As he imagines walking past the candy story he repeats over and over with a smile, "I'm not going to eat sugar today so that I can concentrate well and graduate from high school." He repeats the statement and holds the image until his belief feels totally true. He then tells an empowering story of what it's like to release sugar from his life.

After several sessions, Sean deepens the healing by repeating the process with a more intense trigger: an actual chocolate bar, which he holds in his hand and smells. Then when he repeats his empowering statement with his empowering image, he smells the chocolate at the same time. This creates a powerful situation since the trigger is more intense. Even with this more intense trigger, Sean eventually is able to smell the chocolate without triggering a craving. After a total of nine sessions, Sean becomes fully desensitized to the smell or sight of chocolate.

Be Mindful of Emotional Reactions on a Regular Basis
Throughout each day – at home, at school and with friends – Sean checks in with himself periodically for any unpleasant emotional reactions, especially sugar cravings. When these arise, he immediately applies the Focus on Everything technique, and stays with it until the reaction or craving fully dissolves.

Make Unified Mindfulness a Regular Part of Your Life Sean spends 10–15 minutes a day formally practising the Focus on Everything technique. He does this first thing in the morning, right after waking up.

He experiences many additional positive life changes. He starts to get excellent grades in school. He wins a student-of-the-month award and graduates from high school. After two years, upon follow-up, Sean stated that he eats a small amount of sugar occasionally but without bingeing.

ADDICTION SCENARIO #4: KICKING THE CHEWING TOBACCO HABIT (OLDER PROTOCOL)

Peter has a long-standing chewing tobacco addiction. He has tried many types of therapies in an attempt to give it up but has not had any success so far. He feels great distress about his addiction because his children are upset about it and he is also acutely aware of the carcinogenic aspect of the habit. What makes things worse is that one of his co-workers also chews tobacco and constantly offers it to him at his workplace.

Step 1: Identify the Issue and Choose an Empowering Statement Peter is a chewing tobacco addict engaging in the habit several times per day. For his empowering statement, Peter chooses, "I'm not going to chew tobacco today because I want to be alive for my sons' weddings."

Step 2: Choose a Trigger Peter chooses an empty can of chewing tobacco for his trigger. He prefers not to use the real thing, but this trigger works well because he can still smell the tobacco.

Step 3: Apply Exposure and Desensitization Peter smells the empty can of chewing tobacco during his first session and immediately triggers a craving of 10. He applies the exposure and desensitization and his craving gradually drops to 5. At the end of the next round of exposure and desensitization his craving is 0. He attempts to trigger the craving again and this time his craving level is lower at a 3. By the end of the first session, Peter cannot trigger the craving. He moves on to Step 4.

Step 4: Choose an Image or Scenario that Represents the Worst Possible Consequences of the Addiction Peter chooses a disturbing scenario of one of his sons' wedding and his absence. He holds the image while he repeats his empowering statement, "I'm not going to chew tobacco today because I want to be here for my sons' weddings." He repeats the statement and holds the consequential image until it feels completely true. He then tells a story about the consequences of his chewing tobacco habit. He then moves on to Step 5.

Step 5: Choose an Empowering image and Hold it in Your Mind with the Empowering Statement Peter chooses an empowering image of himself saying "no" to his co-worker who offers him chewing tobacco at the workplace. He holds the image in his mind as he repeats his empowering statement, "I'm not going to chew tobacco today because I want to be alive for my sons' weddings." He repeats the statement three times while holding the image until it feels completely true. He then tells an empowering story about his life without chewing tobacco.

Peter became free of his chewing tobacco addiction after only five sessions. He stated how he never believed that he would ever be able to give it up completely.

Be Mindful of Emotional Reactions on a Regular Basis Peter maintained a daily Unified Mindfulness practice and was quite motivated to do so. He discussed the usefulness of applying the techniques to emotional reactions as well as regularly making use of his empowering statements.

Make Unified Mindfulness a Regular Part of Your Life Peter integrated mindfulness into his daily life and reported its positive effect on every aspect of living. He discussed having improved communication with his wife and children, as well as better management of work-related stress.

SUMMARY

- The UMED Process can be greatly helpful in resolving a wide range of addictive behaviours.
- In some cases, the UMED Process can also generate an aversion to a previously addictive substance or behaviour.
- The Release and Empowerment Protocol for Overcoming Negative Behaviours is a variation of the UMED Process that is particularly effective for unwinding addiction and impulse control disorders.

CHAPTER 14

UNWINDING OBSESSIVE-COMPULSIVE DISORDER AND IMPULSE CONTROL ISSUES

So far, I've demonstrated how the Unified Mindfulness Exposure and Desensitization Process can help people who are suffering from anxiety, panic and addiction effectively transform these conditions. I've also presented a variation of the UMED Process – the Release and Empowerment Protocol for Overcoming Negative Behaviours – designed specifically to help people overcome addiction and other negative behaviours.

In this chapter, I'll be presenting scenarios involving people who are struggling with obsessive-compulsive disorder (OCD) or impulse control issues. In each of these cases, we'll see how the UMED Process is used to facilitate emotional repair and restore psychological balance.

OCD is a condition in which people feel driven to do something repetitively, or repeatedly experience intrusive and unwanted thoughts – often in ways that disrupt their lives and create immense suffering. If you or someone you're familiar with has OCD, then you know from direct experience the kind of difficulties this entails day to day.

But there is reason for hope. Like anxiety and panic, the dysfunctional patterns associated with OCD can be effectively unwound via the UMED Process, allowing a return to a more relaxed, enjoyable and effective way of inhabiting one's life.*

SCENARIO #1: IRRATIONAL FEAR OF SKIN-WALKERS

Lara is a 25-year-old Navajo woman who lives on a reservation, and who is studying to become a film-maker. She has struggled with OCD for as long as she can remember.

When she was young, Lara had a hand-washing compulsion. She would wash her hands more than 20 times a day. She became free of this particular compulsion when she was a teenager, but her OCD has continued to express itself in other ways.

Most recently, she has become obsessed with skin-walkers. Some aspects of traditional Navajo culture entail a belief in these powerfully malevolent witches. Skin-walkers have the ability to disguise themselves as animals, possess people and force the people they've possessed to harm – or even kill – other human beings.

One complicating factor is that Lara's relatives firmly embrace such beliefs. This adds to her fearful obsession with skin-walkers. This obsession now seriously disrupts Lara's life. She obsessively fears that a skin-walker will appear, possess her and make her do evil things.

When Lara hears sounds outside her bedroom window at night, she believes that skin-walkers are hiding outside. When she takes a walk near her house, she thinks skin-walkers are hovering in the shadows, stalking her. If a dog runs past her, she believes it is a skin-walker in disguise. When she sees a

---

* Pilot study: A university psychology department performed a statistical analysis on Shelly Young's clinical data collected from individuals with an OCD diagnosis. Using a repeated measures ANOVA, based on the standard OCI scale (Obsessive-Compulsive Inventory), a significant recovery effect was identified.

reflection in a window, she feels that skin-walkers are watching her. Because of these obsessive fears, Lara stops attending classes and leaves her home less often. She is miserable much of the time.

Now let's look at how Lara uses the UMED Process to successfully dissolve her OCD. As you'll see, because her suffering is so severe, the entire healing process takes some time: 35 sessions over several months. But after just a few sessions, she is able to resume attending classes. And, by the end of the process, her OCD is gone.

Step 1: Identify the Issue Lara's primary issue – the most painful and debilitating expression of her OCD – is her extreme fear of skin-walkers.

Step 2: Choose a Trigger Lara chooses to work with an internal trigger. She imagines a mini-scenario in which she is taken over by a skin-walker, hurts people and feels cold and uncaring toward them.

Step 3: Identify the Negative Belief Lara's negative belief is: *I'm afraid of being negatively influenced by skin-walkers.*

Step 4: Create a Realistic Empowering Statement After a little reflection, Lara comes up with this empowering, realistic statement: *I have never been influenced by skin-walkers and I never will be.* (Partway through her healing process, Lara changes this to: *I have never been influenced by skin-walkers and I never will be because they don't exist.* After further sessions, she changes it again, to: *Thoughts about skin-walkers have no power over me.*)

Step 5: Apply the Exposure and Desensitization Process Lara vividly imagines herself being taken over by a skin-walker, hurting people and feeling cold and uncaring toward them. It takes only about five seconds of her playing this mental video to strongly activate her fear of skin-walkers. Lara rates her level of disturbance as 10.

Now Lara applies the Unified Mindfulness Focus Out technique – noting and labeling external sights and sounds, as well as non-emotional physical sensations. She uses the technique for a few minutes, then rates her disturbance level again. Now it is 5.

Lara immediately repeats Step 5 for another 10 minutes, then evaluates her level of suffering again. Now it is 4.

Because Lara's anxiety level starts out so high, she needs 30 sessions, over a five-month period, before the anxiety can no longer be triggered. She then moves on to Step 6.

Step 6: Create an Empowering Scenario For her positive image, Lara creates a mini-scenario of herself moving confidently through her day, undisturbed by any skin-walker thoughts that arise. This is a very wise choice. Lara does *not* envision a life in which such thoughts never arise. That would be unrealistic. Instead, she imagines those thoughts arising *but causing no distress or disruption to her life.*

As she holds this image in mind, Lara smiles gently, enjoying any emotional and physical pleasure that arises, and repeats her positive statement: *I have never been influenced by skin-walkers and I never will be.*

After repeating this empowering statement several times out loud in a calm and confident voice, she once again rates how true this positive statement feels. It is now rated as 9.

From then on, Lara reinforces her healing through the following ongoing practices.

Be Mindful of Emotional Reactions on a Regular Basis As Lara goes through her day, if she notices the beginnings of fear, agitation, anger or paranoia, she stops what she is doing as quickly as she can. Then she applies the Focus Out technique and stays with it until the sensations mostly or completely dissolve.

Make Unified Mindfulness a Regular Part of Your Life
Lara enthusiastically commits to a formal Unified Mindfulness practice in which she uses the Focus Out technique for 15–20 minutes each day. Over time, she gradually increases this amount of time until she regularly practices this form of Unified Mindfulness for 45–60 minutes per day. She also repeats her empowering statement, which she keeps in an easily accessible location on her phone and tablet, several times a day. After one and half years, Lara is working on other issues with her therapist. The skin-walkers issue has been completely resolved.

SCENARIO #2: COMPULSIVE HAIR PULLING

Cindy is a 27-year-old woman who suffers from trichotillomania, a compulsion to pull on – and pull out – her hair. Here is how Cindy moves through the UMED Process, fully healing from this challenging condition within three months.

Step 1: Identify the Issue Cindy's obvious issue is compulsive hair pulling.

Step 2: Choose a Trigger Cindy spends some time considering and making a list of the many possible triggers. She decides to work with the trigger of touching her head.

Step 3: Identify the Negative Belief After some reflection, Cindy realizes that her issue is about more than just the hair-pulling itself. She also suffers from this negative belief: *I'm a failure because I have this compulsion to pull out my hair.*

Step 4: Create a Realistic Empowering Statement Cindy settles on this positive statement: *Trichotillomania is a psychological disorder that has nothing to do with my success or failure.*

Step 5: Apply the Exposure and Desensitization Process Cindy applies her trigger: she holds her fingers against her head until the compulsion to pull her hair is strongly activated. This takes about 20 seconds. Cindy then evaluates her level of disturbance as 6.

Cindy immediately begins practising the Unified Mindfulness Focus Out technique. After using this technique for 10 minutes, she rates her level of suffering once again. Now it is at 2.

Step 6: Create a Realistic Empowering Scenario Cindy creates an empowering mini-scenario in which she feels an urge to pull out her hair but does not act on it – and does not feel any distress from not acting.

As she holds this empowering image in mind, Cindy repeats her empowering statement aloud several times: *Trichotillomania is a psychological disorder that has nothing to do with my success or failure.* At the same time she smiles gently, appreciating any pleasant sensations that arise. Then she rates the felt truth of this positive statement. She gives it 9.

After repeating Step 6 several times, the positive statement feels entirely true to Cindy, and she rates it as 10, three times in a row.

Then, on an ongoing basis, Cindy supports her healing through the following practices.

Be Mindful of Emotional Reactions on a Regular Basis In her daily life, Cindy makes it a point to use the Focus on Everything technique – in particular, the label *feel* – to any unpleasant emotional sensations that arise in her body. As soon as she notices any urge to pull out her hair, she applies the technique and stays with it until the urge disappears.

Cindy experiences complete freedom from the trichotillomania behaviour after a few sessions and complete freedom from the urge after 12 sessions. She then moves on to work with other issues in therapy.

Make Unified Mindfulness a Regular Part of Your Life Cindy adopts a formal mindfulness practice, employing the Focus Out technique for 15–20 minutes, twice per day: once in the morning and once in the evening. In addition, she writes her positive statement on the back of one of her business cards and carries it with her. She repeats this statement, either out loud or to herself, several times each day, *feeling* it to be *true*.

SUMMARY

- The UMED Process is a powerful tool for unwinding a wide range of obsessive-compulsive disorders and impulse control disorders.
- Even if you've been suffering for years or decades with OCD or an impulse control issue, the UMED Process may help to resolve the suffering very quickly.
- The positive statement you create in Step 4 can evolve over time as part of your healing process.

CHAPTER 15

HEALING TRAUMA

The final form of psychological disturbances that we'll consider are those that result from trauma. It's unusual to find someone who hasn't experienced some form of trauma at some point in their life – whether mild or severe, chronic or acute, individual or collective. So, if you are a survivor of a traumatic event, the first thing to understand is that you're not alone. And the second thing to know is that the UMED Process can help you unwind the disturbing and disruptive effects of the traumatic experience and restore a sense of wellbeing and psychological harmony.

Now, let's consider trauma a bit more closely. What, exactly, is it? Most basically, when an experience exceeds our capacity to fully digest it in that particular moment, it registers in our mind–body as trauma.

Many traumatizing experiences are physically or emotionally extreme: being robbed at gunpoint; learning that someone you care about has been killed; becoming seriously injured yourself; seeing live action as a soldier in a brutal military campaign; being sexually assaulted; or surviving an earthquake or other natural disaster.

But it's also possible to experience trauma from a seemingly insignificant event. A healthy, happy young boy who momentarily wanders away from his mother on a crowded street might feel traumatized by the panic of losing sight of her, even for just 30 seconds. A healthy, stable adult who hears a loud and unexpected sound – say, the explosion of a firecracker half a block away – may also experience a trauma response. The mind–body does not always react logically. It may not make a distinction between that small explosion and the sound of gunfire. And, no matter what its cause, the trauma can lead to deep and persistent anxiety and insecurity.

Unified Mindfulness techniques can help us skillfully, and more completely, digest our moment-by-moment experience in ways that prevent it from congealing into trauma. They can also help us heal the scars of trauma that have already formed in our mind–bodies. The examples that I present here will show you how this kind of deep healing and transformation can be achieved.

TRAUMA SCENARIO #1: HELLS ANGELS AND HYPERVIGILANCE

Joseph is a 50-year-old man who experiences post-traumatic stress disorder (PTSD). His symptoms include severe anxiety, hyper-vigilance and frequent flashbacks. These symptoms are related to Joseph's violent past as an outlaw biker with the Hells Angels. Even though he abandoned the Angels and the outlaw lifestyle long ago, their effects linger in his life.

After years of alcohol and methamphetamine abuse, Joseph is now completely clean and sober. Nevertheless, his PTSD prevents him from living a normal life. He is afraid to leave his house, checks around his car before getting in it and is constantly on guard for fear of being murdered by enemies of the Hells Angels.

Here is how Joseph uses the UMED Process to support the unwinding of his PTSD symptoms.

Step 1: Identify the Issue The specific issue Joseph begins with is his fear that a bomb will explode when he opens his mailbox.

Step 2: Choose a Trigger Joseph chooses to work with a mini-scenario of him opening his mailbox and a bomb detonating a moment later.

Step 3: Identify the Negative Belief The negative belief here is clear: *I'm terrified that a bomb will go off when I open my mailbox.*

Step 4: Create a Realistic Empowering Statement Joseph understands not to replace his negative belief with: *It's very unlikely that someone will put a bomb in my mailbox,* because that fear is not entirely unrealistic. He knows who his old enemies are – and he also knows that they are capable of putting bombs in people's mailboxes. Wisely, Joseph avoids wishful and magical thinking, and settles on this positive statement: *Ultimately, I have no control over life and death – and neither does anyone else – but that's okay.* This is a bold and straightforward acknowledgment of the human condition.

Step 5: Apply the Exposure and Desensitization Process Joseph vividly imagines a bomb exploding as he opens his mailbox. He plays and replays this mental video for five seconds, until fear wells up inside him. He then rates his disturbance level as 8.

Now Joseph applies the Focus on Rest technique for 10 minutes. Afterwards, he again rates his level of fear and distress, this time as 5.

Without pausing, Joseph goes through Step 5 again several times over a period of several sessions. Then he evaluates his disturbance level. It has dropped to 0. He feels he is ready to move on to Step 6.

Step 6: Create an Empowering Scenario Joseph chooses a mini-scenario in which he calmly walks to the mailbox, opens it and takes out a stack of mail, being mindful of any emotional reaction.

While holding in mind this empowering image, Joseph repeats his empowering statement: *Ultimately, I have no control over life and death, and neither does anyone else, but that's okay.* At the same time, he appreciates any pleasant emotional and physical sensations that arise.

Joseph now evaluates how true this positive statement feels. This time, and the next two times he completes Step 6 too, he rates its felt truth as 10.

Note that Joseph's empowering statement and empowering image are quite different. That's okay. A positive *statement* needs to be realistic. But a positive *image* simply has to be believable and reasonable. Joseph would be unwise to *believe* that none of his old enemies would ever try to hurt him. But it's not unwise for him to *envision* himself getting his mail without being harmed.

Thereafter, Joseph continues to support his healing through the ongoing practices.

Be Mindful of Emotional Reactions on a Regular Basis
As Joseph goes through his day, he notes any unpleasant emotional sensations in his body, especially anxiety or hyper-vigilance. As soon as they arise, he applies the Focus on Rest or Focus on Everything technique – or, occasionally, both – until the sensations mostly or completely dissolve.

Make Unified Mindfulness a Regular Part of Your Life
Joseph commits to a formal mindfulness practice in which he uses the Focus on Rest technique, which can be especially helpful for people with PTSD. He practises this technique for

10–15 minutes twice a day. If, during the night, he wakes up feeling anxious, he practises Focus on Rest for another 10–15 minutes while lying in bed.

To deepen his healing, he also writes down his positive statement on a sheet of paper, which he puts on his refrigerator door. He repeats this statement, either out loud or to himself, frequently throughout the day – each time until it *feels* true.

Joseph experiences a significant decrease in his PTSD symptoms. He loses his fear of leaving the house and lands a fulfilling volunteer job at a local animal shelter. He pursues more self-employment and develops greater financial stability.

TRAUMA SCENARIO #2: TWO SUICIDES AND SEXUAL ABUSE

Patrick is 48 years old, unemployed and living on Social Security disability benefits. He has severe PTSD symptoms, including nightmares and flashbacks, which are primarily related to traumatic events much earlier in his life.

In 1978, when he was 16, Patrick and some friends were cleaning guns together. His best friend Simon began to play Russian roulette – and shot himself in the head. Simon died a day later.

A week after witnessing this suicide, Patrick was sexually molested by a friend of the family, who recognized Patrick's vulnerability.

Over the course of the following year, Patrick was repeatedly molested by this same man, who also forced Patrick to take a variety of psychoactive drugs, including LSD and PCP. As is often the case with such abuse, the family "friend" told Patrick that he or a family member would be killed if he mentioned the abuse to anyone.

Soon afterwards Patrick began to drink, using alcohol to mask his PTSD symptoms. By the time he graduated from high school his drinking had become full-blown alcoholism.

Eventually, Patrick found his way to Alcoholics Anonymous. He found an AA sponsor with whom he formed a deeply healing bond. For over a year, Patrick's sponsor, Art, assisted him in his recovery. The two would frequently meet for coffee, often in one of their homes.

Then, one day, when Patrick came home and opened his garage door, he discovered Art inside – dead, hanging by his neck from a rope.

This sight did more than just trigger Patrick's PTSD. The depression that followed put him in hospital.

When Patrick returned home, he could not bring himself to go into his garage to smoke a cigarette, which was his usual routine. He could not even look at the garage door, which had indentations where Art's flailing legs had kicked it as he died.

When Patrick begins working with the UMED Process, he routinely has flashbacks of being molested, of watching his friend Simon kill himself and of finding his sponsor hanging dead in his garage.

Here's how Patrick uses the UMED Process to support his healing.

Step 1: Identify the Issue Patrick wants to address his post-traumatic stress disorder – especially his nightmares, recurring flashbacks and his inability to enter his garage to smoke a cigarette.

Step 2: Choose a Trigger Patrick makes a list of all the things that trigger his PTSD symptoms. It's a long list. Patrick chooses to work with four: his inability to enter his garage where he witnessed the hanging; flashback images; nightmare images; and a photo of the indentations in his garage door.

Step 3: Identify the Negative Belief It takes Patrick some time to discover what his negative beliefs are. Eventually he realizes that he feels guilty about Art's death – and perhaps, somehow, even partly responsible for it. Patrick expresses this as: *I should have done more to help Art.* Patrick understands how untrue that negative belief actually is, but it haunts him nevertheless.

Step 4: Create a Realistic Empowering Statement Patrick settles on this positive statement: *I knew he was dead as soon as I saw him. I could not have done more. I forgive myself.*

Step 5: Apply the Exposure and Desensitization Process Patrick completes Step 5 many times, alternating among the four triggers. He holds a trigger image in his mind until he begins experiencing strong disturbance. This takes only a few seconds.

The first time Patrick does Step 5, he measures his disturbance level as 10.

Patrick then applies a mindfulness technique for a few minutes. He decides to use three different Unified Mindfulness techniques: Focus on Rest, Focus Out and Focus on Everything. Each time he does Step 5, he chooses whatever technique feels right to him in that moment.

Over time, and with multiple repetitions of Step 5, his level of disturbance shrinks from 10 to 3 to 1, and eventually to 0.

Step 6: Create a Realistic Empowering Scenario For his empowering image, Patrick initially chooses a mental image of Art looking him in the eye and letting him know that he did the best he could and could not have done more.

Patrick repeats Step 6 many times. Sometimes he uses his mental image of Art; sometimes he uses a similar mental image of his teenage friend Simon.

While holding one of these empowering images in mind, Patrick repeats his empowering statement multiple times: *I knew he was dead as soon as I saw him. I could not have done more. I forgive myself.* At the same time, he smiles and appreciates any relief or release that arises.

Over time, and after many repetitions, the felt truth of Patrick's positive statement goes up to 9 and then to 10.

From then on, in support of his healing, Patrick does the following practices.

Be Mindful of Emotional Reactions on a Regular Basis

Throughout his day, Patrick does his best to note unpleasant emotional sensations as soon as they arise – and then to immediately apply the Focus on Rest or Focus on Everything technique, until the sensations mostly or completely dissolve.

Patrick also uses one or more Unified Mindfulness techniques whenever a flashback begins. This prevents fear, anxiety and other forms of suffering from becoming overwhelming.

Make Unified Mindfulness a Regular Part of Your Life

Patrick employs a mindfulness technique any time he plans to enter his garage. He starts using the technique a few minutes beforehand and continues using it until he leaves the garage and shuts the door behind him. He uses all three of his chosen techniques – Focus on Rest, Focus Out and Focus on Everything – each time choosing the one that feels right at that moment.

The UMED Process does not magically make Patrick symptom-free. It does, however, make his flashbacks fewer and much more manageable. He also has fewer nightmares. After three months of this healing work, he is able to go into his garage to smoke a cigarette at any time without fear or anxiety.

After about four months of practise – including 20+ UMED Process sessions – Patrick experiences only one or two nightmares or flashbacks per month. He now feels confident in his ability to successfully apply a mindfulness technique to any flashback or nightmare that arises. Because of the UMED Process, Patrick says, "I got my life back."

SUMMARY

- The UMED Process offers powerful support for the healing of trauma and the processing of overwhelming reactions.
- No matter how overwhelming and extensive the mental and emotional effects of trauma may be, they can be effectively addressed through Unified Mindfulness techniques.
- The Focus on Rest technique can be especially helpful for people who wake up during the night with PTSD symptoms.

CHAPTER 16

ALTERNATE ROUTES

If you observe how a small stream makes its way down a mountainside, you'll notice that its path is organically, naturally, the most efficient one – but is never perfectly straight. The stream rushes and pools, meanders and cascades, turns and flows in response to the various obstacles that it encounters. It keeps moving, but never in a rigidly linear, unswerving fashion. Its innate intelligence – rather than any preconceived ideas – guides its way.

And the same is true of our journey through life and, more specifically, with the application of any healing modality. The UMED Process has proven itself to be profoundly effective for many people. It's for this reason that I encourage you to follow all the practices and steps in this book, if you can.

But the UMED Process is not a one-size-fits-all solution. Every human being is unique, and no one approach to healing works for every person every time.

It's possible that one or more of the mindfulness methods presented in this book won't make a positive difference for you. Or perhaps you'll find a particular activity difficult or impossible to practise. Not everyone needs every step of the UMED Process in order to heal. In a clinical setting, people sometimes make a sudden leap forward, skipping right over a part of the usual process – and still fully heal. Others need to repeat and linger, taking longer to absorb and fully benefit from a particular stage of the process.

So, it's always possible to take an alternate route: to lengthen, shorten or revise the steps of the UMED Process to respond with greatest intelligence and sensitivity to your own or a client's unique circumstances. This kind of intuitive flexibility is something that I honour and encourage.

That said, if you do take an alternate route, I would recommend that you follow these general guidelines:

- If you skip something, continue to follow the overall process presented in this book. Don't jump backward and forward from one chapter to another.
- Make a note of whatever practice you've skipped. Then try returning to it a few days, weeks or even months later, and see if it works for you now. If it does, wonderful. If it doesn't, let it go.
- If you find one specific practice, step, technique, empowering statement or scenario especially helpful, feel free to use it over and over.
- The Unified Mindfulness methods presented in Chapters 3–8 can be deeply and profoundly transformational. Please do as many of these as you can.
- In Chapter 10, which introduces the six steps of the UMED Process, Step 5 – the exposure and desensitization process – is especially valuable. If you can be with any trigger or stimulus until your level of disturbance shrinks to 0, even just once, this alone can make a notable difference in terms of emotional repair. And if you can hold an empowering statement and scenario in your mind (steps 4 and 6) – even only once – this, too, can be greatly helpful.

Unified Mindfulness is ultimately about freedom. If any practice in this book tightens rather than loosens a problem that binds you, then I encourage you to drop that practice, skip over it and continue moving forward.

And please keep this in mind: if you don't complete the full UMED Process – and, as a result, you experience some improvement but not complete healing – you are still much better off than you were before you encountered these Unified Mindfulness methods. You now have powerful tools to help you cultivate concentration, clarity and equanimity – three genuine treasures that can and will continue to enhance your wellbeing for years to come.

SUMMARY

- The UMED Process is not a one-size-fits-all solution. Every human being is unique, and no one approach to healing works for every person every time.
- Honour your own intuition and intelligence in choosing which Unified Mindfulness methods to employ.
- The concentration, clarity and equanimity cultivated through mindfulness practice are three genuine treasures that will benefit you for years to come.

PART THREE

THE END OF ALL STORIES

Already, it's been a beautiful journey. In Part One, you learned a variety of valuable Unified Mindfulness techniques – each one equipped to cultivate concentration, clarity and equanimity. With these mindfulness methods in tow, you were then prepared to enter the territory of the UMED Process in Part Two – applying those methods, along with exposure and desensitization protocols, to specific psychological challenges. You experienced first-hand how the UMED Process facilitates emotional repair and supports psychological wellness, and deepened your understanding through a series of inspirational case studies and scenarios.

So, what lies *beyond* emotional repair? Is there another leg of the journey – another peak or valley or winding river to explore? **Chapter 17** – our final chapter – answers this question by exploring the freedom within and beyond all stories.

You may recall from the case study I shared in this book's introduction that one of my favourite phrases is: "Suffering is always decreased when the story is released." Learning to let go of the mind's conceptual narratives is a great way to reduce psychological suffering and access our inherent freedom.

But as it turns out, freedom is to be found not only *beyond* but also *within* all such stories. If this sounds paradoxical … well, it is, and deliciously so! The Absolute Activity exercises presented in this chapter provide a way for you to explore this paradox.

You see, from the perspective of the world's contemplative traditions, mental illness is often considered – ultimately – to be just a matter of degree. How so? From this point of view, anyone who has not yet gained insight into the radical impermanence of their body and mind and clarified their true identity – whether or not they have a psychiatric diagnosis – is in some sense mentally ill. In other words, emotional repair of psychological imbalance is only half of the story, only part of the journey to genuine, lasting sanity.

In its combination of Unified Mindfulness methods with powerful exposure and desensitization protocols and cognitive behavioural techniques, the UMED Process is designed not only to facilitate emotional repair and relieve suffering, but also to enhance wellbeing at ordinary and extraordinary levels.

Here, in our final chapter, you'll be reminded that the source of true and lasting happiness is an inner peace that arises out of the wisdom of your true nature and remains forever independent of physical, mental, emotional or worldly circumstances. This is the Holy Grail of both psychological healing and spiritual insight. It's the discovery of your essential identity as the unlimited indestructible freedom that lies within and beyond all stories.

So (returning to the question with which we began), what lies beyond emotional repair? The answer is both ordinary and extraordinary levels of wellbeing and fulfillment characterized by genuine contentment, causeless joy and authentically self-expressive movement of your precious human body–mind through your chosen world.

CHAPTER 17

FREEDOM WITHIN AND BEYOND ALL STORIES

"We shall not cease from exploration
And the end of all our exploring
Will be to arrive where we started
And know the place for the first time. "

TS Eliot*

We began our exploration (in this book's first pages) with an invitation to adopt a playful, curious and inquisitive attitude; to create a gentle inner smile; and to allow the energy of that smile to permeate your entire body-mind. I hope you've carried this attitude and simple practice with you and returned to it again and again as you journeyed through the chapters.

Now, let's review a bit of what you've learned – and tease out some of its liberating implications and avenues for further exploration.

---

* Excerpt from "Little Gidding" in *Four Quartets*, Houghton Mifflin Harcourt: 1968.

SELF-STORIES AND SUFFERING

Throughout this book I've pointed out, again and again, how psychological suffering has everything to do with the way we relate to our self-story – the ever-changing weave of thoughts, images and emotions that constitute our psychological self.

When we fixate on this psychological self – when we assume it to be a permanent, separate, unchanging entity that we strongly identify with – then we tend to suffer. Why? Because this assumption of an unchanging individual self is at odds with the ever-transforming nature of all phenomena, including our thoughts, images and feelings, which make up our mental–emotional experience. In the same way that the elements of the natural world are in constant flux and flow, so are the elements of sensory experience.

Though we may be in the habit of saying that we "experience suffering," it would actually be more accurate to say that we "suffer our experience." When we relate to the arising and dissolving of phenomena – our *experience* of "self" and "world" – via the assumption of an unchanging, limited, separate self, we inevitably "suffer our experience." As a result, our relationship with phenomena will be fraught with conflict and inner tension.

But when we see more clearly what's actually going on we become able, quite naturally, to *witness* our experience; to *embrace* that experience; to more often *enjoy* our experience; and, in many cases, to playfully *create* and *transform* our experience. Mindfulness practice is a potent tool for catalyzing just such a transformation and you now have some truly excellent Unified Mindfulness methods to support your own healing process.

THE MIRACLE OF MINDFULNESS

What gives mindfulness its unique power?

Through mindfulness practice, we're able to cultivate increasing levels of concentration, clarity and equanimity. We become able to see more clearly what's actually happening, and to relate more skillfully to the arising and dissolving of the strands of sensory experience that constitute "self" and "world." We're able and willing to experience things just as they are – without denying parts of our experience or superimposing something extra.

As we've seen in previous chapters, Unified Mindfulness techniques can be used to support psychological healing and transform behaviour in the direction of greater peace, joy, harmony, wisdom and intelligence.

DISENTANGLING, SOAKING AND OPENING

The power of our mindfulness practice arises via its two main activities: 1) disentangling and 2) soaking and opening. So far, I've emphasized the disentangling aspect of mindfulness because of its vital role in releasing psychological suffering. With our noting and labeling techniques, we **disentangle** thoughts, images, feelings and perceptions, like loosening a dense knot. We invite and notice the spaciousness between, around and within these various strands of experience.

We then imagine or feel the phenomena being **soaked** in awareness and **opened**, dissolved or rendered transparent. We notice that our *experience* of phenomena and our *awareness of* this experience are inseparable – which is how things actually are. The strands of sensory experience arise and dissolve within the field of awareness like clouds passing through a vast blue sky. While the clouds come and go, the sky remains.

DISENTANGLE AND BE FREE

Returning to the archetypes I touched on at the beginning of the book (see page xxxiii), if you are inspired by the warrior archetype, you might refer to this process as a *divide-and-conquer* strategy for winning the war against ignorance and suffering. If you resonate more easily with artists, alchemists, detectives or chess masters, you might describe this process as a most ingenious *disentangle-and-be-free* game plan.

Whichever metaphor you like the most, the idea is the same: what was once experienced as an overwhelming and hopelessly complex challenge becomes much more manageable by dividing it into its constituent parts.

When you clearly perceive how self-stories and world-stories are created, maintained, protected/defended and then dissolved, their power to trigger psychological suffering is greatly reduced. You can skillfully disentangle them, creatively transform them and allow them naturally to dissolve or become fully transparent to the awareness that is their unchanging background.

APPRECIATE, TRANSCEND, NURTURE AND EXPRESS

A skillfully embraced mindfulness practice allows you to: appreciate "self" and "world" more fully; to transcend "self" and "world"; to nurture positivity; to compassionately improve both "self" and "world"; to express spontaneity; and to experience radical freedom and creativity. How wonderful!

With mindfulness, you learn to embrace the phenomena of your experience with increased intimacy, appreciating and enjoying them more fully. You also come to understand and know yourself more clearly at all levels: at the level of your human body; at the various levels of your psychological self; and at your most essential, transpersonal, non-phenomenal level – as primordial perfection.

The fruit of this insight is the ability to be simultaneously free and skillfully engaged within your self-story, like an actor playing a role in a theatrical production. At the same time, you knowingly abide in the space beyond all stories – the place of your truest identity and unconditioned freedom.

ABSOLUTE REST AND ABSOLUTE ACTIVITY

The Unified Mindfulness techniques introduced in this book are mostly about learning to *improve* and more fully *appreciate* "self" and "world." Hopefully, you've experienced for yourself how these methods can be used to transform mental and emotional imbalances – so improving the quality of your moment-by-moment experience and restoring your capacity to deeply appreciate your human life.

Another aspect of Unified Mindfulness is *transcending* "self" and "world," and accessing a wholly transpersonal and non-phenomenal dimension of experience. The poet TS Eliot alludes to such a dimension as a *still point* and contrasts it with *the dance* of worldly phenomena (see page 65).

Unified Mindfulness acknowledges this still point – and the dance – as well, but with the terms *absolute rest* and *absolute activity*. As you learned in Chapter 4 (in a special adjunct to the Focus on Rest technique) *absolute rest* is what arises – or, more precisely, what is unveiled – when a sensory experience disappears and nothing replaces it. And *absolute activity* is defined as effortless expansion and contraction. Each of these can be accessed with the support of mindfulness practice.

THE DANCE: FLOWING EMPTINESS

You've already explored the "still point" of absolute rest (see Chapter 4, pages 66–67). Now let's take a closer look at "the dance" of absolute activity. You may be wondering why I've waited until this final chapter of the book to introduce absolute activity.

This is because absolute activity tends to arise *spontaneously* once we've resolved a good portion of the internal resistance that characterizes psychological suffering. Now that you've been introduced – in the book's previous chapters – to Unified Mindfulness techniques designed to resolve such internal resistance, learning about absolute activity is a natural next step.

When a person is struggling with a particular mental–emotional disharmony, it's best to first employ one of the Unified Mindfulness methods described in Chapters 4–8 and/or the UMED Process discussed at length in Part Two to resolve this disturbance. Once the psychological suffering has been mostly or entirely disentangled, you'll be able to more easily engage with these absolute activity explorations. In other words, you'll be able to access and fully appreciate the dance of flowing emptiness.

Does this mean that having access to absolute rest and absolute activity *requires* a full resolution of any and all psychological imbalances? Not at all. For some people, tuning into the transpersonal dimension of absolute rest and absolute activity may be possible even in the midst of challenging mental–emotional disharmonies. However, for most people, resolving such challenges opens the way for a more direct and sustained encounter with absolute rest and absolute activity.

EFFORTLESS EXPANSION AND CONTRACTION

As mentioned, absolute activity can be described as *effortless expansion and contraction*. But what exactly does this mean? This phrase is shorthand for a process that can occur anywhere, at any time:

- *Expansion* refers to the appearance of phenomena – the arising of mental activity and sensory experience; and *contraction* is the dissolution of such phenomena, their disappearance. This is happening all the time, though not always clearly perceived.
- *Effortless* doesn't mean passive or resigned but, rather, free from any internal grasping or resistance. It means that the sensory channels are fully conductive – functioning with equanimity.

As you've already experienced – via the exploration in Chapter 4 – absolute rest is a vibrantly awake *no-thing-ness*. It's what remains when you've let go of sights, sounds, tastes, smells, feelings and thoughts.

Absolute activity, then, is the *flow* of this no-thing-ness. It's any activity – any physical movement, speech or thought – that is free from internal resistance and infused with the energy and awareness of absolute rest. Such activity is often spontaneous, creative and authentically response-able.

Consider an athlete or musician who is "in the zone." Their movements are both vibrant and relaxed: effortlessly precise, responding perfectly to the circumstances. Their playing is infused with creative genius – with an intelligence and energy that seems to come from "somewhere else." This is one example of absolute activity.

Absolute rest and absolute activity are interdependent partners, not opposites. When the belief in a personal separate self has been released, the body and mind become free to function in the mode of emptiness – of thoughts, sensations and perceptions arising and dissolving without any internal resistance, without grasping or repulsion.

This partnership of mental activity and sensory phenomena organically emerging from the source of absolute rest is sometimes called *emptiness dancing*. It's also known as the essential nonduality of emptiness and appearances. Here, nonduality means that the apparent separation between emptiness (*no-thing-ness*) and phenomena (the *appearance* of thoughts, sensations and perceptions) is not ultimately real.

This passage from nonduality guide John Wheeler expresses a bit of the fluidity and freedom of absolute activity:

"Life goes on. There are events, decisions and things to work out. The whole universe is a vast sea of activity, after all. However, the sense of having personal problems disappears. There is just the mind and body functioning in the light of intelligence. Things go a certain way or not, but the concern over the outcome is gone. There can be tremendous care and intelligence applied. All the thoughts and feelings go on just fine. But taking things personally goes.

So, personal suffering, doubt, confusion, anxiety and so forth are left behind. The reason is that the separate person who previously owned or identified with things is removed from the picture. It has nothing to do with the outer events or situations."*

---

*   *Shining in Plain View*, Non-Duality Press: 2005

To help you better understand – and then directly experience – absolute activity, here's a fun experiment, followed by a guided exploration.

EXPERIMENT: MARBLE IN A BOWL

For this experiment you will need a medium-sized bowl and a marble or a very smooth and perfectly round stone. You can use a mixing bowl or salad bowl, a Tibetan singing bowl or a bowl-shaped meditation gong, if you have one.

You'll use these in two different ways.

Way #1: The Precarious Balance of Effortful Mindfulness

1. Turn the bowl upside down.
2. Balance the marble or stone on top of it. You'll need to find the very centre of this convex surface in order for the marble to remain balanced.
3. Then, gently nudge the marble to one side or the other – and notice how quickly it rolls off the bowl – like a boulder cascading down the side of a mountain.

This situation is like an effortful mindfulness practice. Deliberately placing our attention in one spot – like balancing the marble – requires a certain amount of effort. It also lacks stability. When our mindfulness is built around deliberate effort, we are easily susceptible to distractions, which can cause us to spin away from our centre.

Way #2: The Effortlessness of Absolute Rest and Activity

In effortful mindfulness, we toggle back-and-forth between deliberate focusing and distraction. But there is also a second way of mindfulness: an organic interplay of absolute rest and absolute activity.

1. Now turn the bowl right side up and place the marble in it. Notice that the marble naturally and effortlessly comes to rest in the very centre of the bowl.
2. Nudge the marble gently to the right or to the left. Notice that after it moves around for a while, it once again naturally settles into the centre of the bowl with ease and stability. The marble first practises absolute activity, then absolute rest.

As your mindfulness practice deepens, it will naturally transition from the first way to the second, from effortful focusing to the effortlessness of absolute rest and activity.

Contemplate these two ways of resting the marble in the bowl to understand the difference between effortful and effortless mindfulness.

GUIDED EXPLORATION:
EXPRESSING SPONTANEITY

Here are two ways for you to experience a taste of absolute activity.

Way #1: The Intuitive Intelligence of Aimless Wandering

1. Begin with the Guided Exploration for Accessing Absolute Rest from Chapter 4 (pages 66–67). Practise this in a spot that is safe, private and free of potential

hazards. This can be either indoors or outdoors.

2. From this mode of absolute rest, stand up slowly and begin to walk around in seemingly aimless wandering – with no specific agenda, no conscious intention and none of the tension that arises with a goal or destination.

3. Be drawn intuitively in one direction, then another. Your movements may be slow or rapid, or (at different moments) both. You might walk in a straight line, or jog in circles or spirals or do a little dance. You may pause your movements briefly to gaze up at the sky or down at a flower, and then continue walking.

4. After 10–15 minutes of this aimless wandering – this relaxed, spontaneous movement – find a place to sit down.

5. For the next few minutes, sit in one place aimlessly. Experience the spacious vibrance of absolute rest.

Way #2: The Dynamic Creativity of Free Writing

1. Beside you, on a level surface, place a pen and a sheet of paper or a journal opened to a blank page. (For this activity, do not use an electronic device.)

2. Practise the Guided Exploration for Accessing Absolute Rest from Chapter 4 (pages 66–67).

3. Then pick up the pen and begin to write freely. Write whatever comes to mind. If you like, you can begin writing with a sentence stem, such as: *What I most want to say right now is ...* or *If ...* or *I remember ...* or *From my heart-of-hearts I know ...* or *What most delights and surprises me ...*

4. Once you've completed that sentence with whatever

> spontaneously arises, you can either continue or write down the sentence stem again and begin anew.
>
> 5. After 10–15 minutes of free writing, put down your pen.
> 6. Sit quietly for another 10 minutes or so, and experience the spacious vibrance of absolute rest.

* * *

Aimless wandering and free writing are two wonderful ways to facilitate absolute activity and to unleash dynamic creativity and spontaneity. I'd encourage you to experiment with them regularly, or whenever the urge and opportunity arise.

As you experience absolute rest more frequently, you'll also come to recognize how absolute activity naturally emerges from it. This recognition is not something you can deliberately accomplish. Instead, it's a delicious fruit that ripens naturally on the tree of your authentic practice.

SELF AND WORLD AS ABSOLUTE ACTIVITY

The still point of absolute rest gives birth to a spontaneous flow of absolute activity. Yet this still point is not a point in time and space but rather a transpersonal dimension that, if you will, *encompasses* and *engenders* time and space in the way that an ocean encompasses and engenders its waves.

Absolute activity includes the human body in an elemental dance *not* separate from the dance of mountains, rivers, trees and stars. This activity also includes the human personality: the psychological self, our story of "who I am in the world right now."

As you've seen – and, I hope, as you've begun to experience – disentangling the strands of sensory experience that constitute our psychological self-story can help us dissolve the sense of a permanent, unchanging separate self. This, in turn, encourages the dissolving of much of the suffering that arises when we hold our circumstances too tightly.

Once your personality – "who I am in the world right now" – is seen for what it actually is (or, more accurately, what it is *not*), then it becomes free to resurrect as spontaneity, flow and emptiness dancing. It becomes an effortless expression of your primordial perfection.

LIFE'S BUBBLING STREAM

It's likely you've heard the classic nursery rhyme: *Row, row, row your boat gently down the stream. Merrily, merrily, merrily, merrily – life is but a dream.* This whimsical children's song carries great wisdom. If we can rest easily upon life's bubbling stream of constant change, fully aware of its ephemeral and dreamlike qualities, this (paradoxically) frees us to enjoy it even more completely, to become more deliciously intimate with each moment.

From the wisdom of absolute rest and absolute activity, we find ourselves fully engaged in life's activities, while simultaneously in touch with the still point of aware presence: a vibrant and indestructible awake-ness at the core of our being, our true identity. We go about our business in the world, knowing that what appear as our human body, as our psychological "self," and as an "external world" are deeply interwoven, one with the other, like braided currents in the same stream – everchanging and eternally fresh and new.

RESOURCES

ONLINE

Shelly Young's website
www.PresentSolutions4u.com
Information on Shelly Young's practice and powerful video and
   written testimonials regarding Unified Mindfulness-centred
   psychotherapy.

Shinzen Young's personal website
www.shinzen.org
Shinzen's teaching schedule, essays, blog posts and more.

SEMA LAB: Sonication Enhanced Mindful Awareness
www.semalab.arizona.edu
Shinzen Young is presently co-directing the SEMA Lab at the
   University of Arizona.

Shinzen's Home Practice Program
http://homepracticeprogram.com
Monthly group conference-call instruction on the full range
   of Unified Mindfulness techniques, along with occasional
   special topics.

Shinzen's Life Practice Program
www.lifepracticeprogram.com
Weekly support for the integration of mindfulness practice into
   daily life, which includes guided instruction and one-on-one

conversations with practitioners around specific issues involving mindfulness in their daily lives.

Unified Mindfulness LLC
https://unifiedmindfulness.com
The official training platform for Shinzen Young's Unified Mindfulness system, which includes a no-cost, no obligation introductory self-paced online interaction CORE training course and a CORE companion book – both appropriate for any experience level.

Brightmind App
www.brightmind.com
Support for learning Unified Mindfulness techniques that are customized to one's unique pace and goals.

Shinzen Young's Facebook Page
www.facebook.com/Shinzendotorg

Mind and Life Institute (MindRxiv)
www.mindandlife.org/mindrxiv
An open archive for research on mind and contemplative practices. Provides a free and publicly accessible platform to which contemplative researchers in the sciences and humanities can upload working papers, preprints, published papers, data and code.

Ron Gutman's TED Talk: The Hidden Power of Smiling (March 2011)
https://www.ted.com/talks/ron_gutman_the_hidden_power_of_smiling?language=en
An inspiring introduction to research demonstrating the biochemical benefits of a simple smile.

Equanimity in Meditation and Contemplative Research

https://www.ncbi.nlm.nih.gov/pmc/articles/PMC4350240/

Moving beyond Mindfulness: Defining Equanimity as an Outcome Measure in Meditation and Contemplative Research. Gaëlle Desbordes, Tim Gard, Elizabeth A Hoge, Britta K Hölzel, Catherine Kerr, Sara W Lazar, Andrew Olendzki, and David R Vago. *Mindfulness* (N Y). 2015 Apr; 6(2): 356–372.

A contemplative science review of equanimity, including psychological, physiological and neuroimaging methods that have been used to assess equanimity, either directly or indirectly.

BOOKS

Bergmann, Uri. *Neurobiological Foundations for EMDR Practice.* New York: Springer Publishing, 2012.

Doidge, Norman. *The Brain That Changes Itself: Stories of Personal Triumph from the Frontiers of Brain Science.* New York: Penguin Publishing, 2007.

Goleman, Daniel and Richard J Davidson. *Altered Traits: Science Reveals How Meditation Changes Your Mind, Brain, and Body.* New York: Avery Publishing, 2018.

Gunaratana, Bhante. *Mindfulness in Plain English.* Somerville, MA: Wisdom Publications, 2015.

Levine, Peter A. *Waking the Tiger: Healing Trauma.* Berkeley, CA: North Atlantic Books, 1997.

Sumano Bikkhu, Ajahn. *The Brightened Mind.* Wheaton, IL: Quest Books, 2011.

Walker, Matthew. *Why We Sleep: Unlocking the Power of Sleep and Dreams.* New York: Simon & Schuster (Scribner Books), 2018.

Wallace, B Alan. *Contemplative Science: Where Buddhism and Neuroscience Converge*. New York: Columbia University Press, 2007.
Westerhoff, Jan. *Twelve Examples of Illusion*. New York: Oxford University Press, 2010.
Young, Shinzen. *The Science of Enlightenment: How Meditation Works*. Boulder, CO: Sounds True, 2016.

ACKNOWLEDGMENTS

I would like to express my deepest gratitude to Shinzen Young, the creator of the Unified Mindfulness system. These powerful techniques, both on their own and as integral components of the UMED therapeutic process, have helped enhance and restore countless lives. As a result of Shinzen's creative genius and passionate commitment to all beings, many individuals who considered their circumstances to be utterly hopeless are today enjoying fulfilling lives.

I also wish to thank Francine Shapiro, the creator of EMDR (Eye Movement Desensitization Reprocessing), for demonstrating the therapeutic potency of exposure and desensitization and for offering a powerful framework for my Unified Mindfulness Exposure and Desensitization Process.

I would like to express my deepest appreciation to Elizabeth Reninger for her insight, creativity and abundant literary skills, which she so generously applied to the creation of this book. Her impeccable ability to integrate a wide range of material and present it in a light and friendly manner is a great gift.

And finally, I am truly grateful to every client I have had the privilege of working with over the past 20 years. You have been genuine inspirations to me, and great support to all who have followed you. Your courageous dedication to healing and transformation has given hope to the next generation of practitioner–clients. It is because of your willingness to end the story of psychological suffering that the therapeutic process did not become a dead end for you but, instead, the beginning of ever-deepening peace and freedom and the unveiling of unconditioned happiness.

My heartfelt thanks to all of you who offered testimonials – whether in writing or in simply how you're now living your lives – which attest to the power of the methods introduced in this book.

– Shelly Young

Many thanks to all those who have supported this project, financially and otherwise. Generous contributions from Frank Foti, Paul Rubell and two anonymous donors laid the financial foundation. Todd Mertz, the Unified Mindfulness community manager, shepherded the intricate process of creating this book in numerous ways. Donald W McCormick, PhD provided invaluable assistance in the crafting of Chapter 10, which presents with clarity and precision the six steps of the UMED Process.

Scott Edelstein, Carol Killman Rosenberg and Joanna Lal, with their editorial wizardry, added immeasurably to the honed and crafted quality of the manuscript. And, finally, many thanks to the entire team at Trigger Publishing for seeing the potential of this book to benefit many – and bringing it to fruition.

– Elizabeth Reninger

TRIGGERHUB IS ONE OF THE MOST ELITE AND SCIENTIFICALLY PROVEN FORMS OF MENTAL HEALTH INTERVENTION

Trigger Publishing is the leading independent mental health and wellbeing publisher in the UK and US. Our collection of bibliotherapeutic books and the power of lived experience change lives forever. Our courageous authors' lived experiences and the power of their stories are scientifically endorsed by independent federal, state and privately funded research in the US. These stories are intrinsic elements in reducing stigma, making those with poor mental health feel less alone, giving them the privacy they need to heal, ensuring they are guided by the essential steps to kick-start their own journeys to recovery, and providing hope and inspiration when they need it most.

Clinical and scientific research conducted by assistant professor Dr Kristin Kosyluk and her highly acclaimed team in the Department of Mental Health Law & Policy at the University of South Florida (USF), as well as complementary research by her peers across the US, has independently verified the power of lived experience as a core component in achieving mental health prosperity. Their findings categorically confirm lived experience as a leading method in treating those struggling with poor mental health by significantly reducing stigma and the time it takes for them to seek help, self-help or signposting if they are struggling.

Delivered through TriggerHub, our unique online portal and smartphone app, we make our library of bibliotherapeutic titles and other vital resources accessible to individuals and organizations anywhere, at any time and with complete privacy, a crucial element of recovery. As such, TriggerHub is the primary recommendation across the UK and US for the delivery of lived experiences.

At Trigger Publishing and TriggerHub, we proudly lead the way in making the unseen become seen. We are dedicated to humanizing mental health, breaking stigma and challenging outdated societal values to create real action and impact. Find out more about our world-leading work with lived experience and bibliotherapy via triggerhub.com, or by joining us on:

🐦 @triggerhub_
ⓕ @triggerhub.org
📷 @triggerhub_

Dr Kristin Kosyluk, PhD, is an assistant professor in the Department of Mental Health Law and Policy at USF, a faculty affiliate of the Louis de la Parte Florida Mental Health Institute, and director of the STigma Action Research (STAR) Lab. Find out more about Dr Kristin Kosyluk, her team and their work by visiting:

USF Department of Mental Health Law & Policy:
www.usf.edu/cbcs/mhlp/index.aspx

USF College of Behavioral and Community Sciences:
www.usf.edu/cbcs/index.aspx

STAR Lab: www.usf.edu/cbcs/mhlp/centers/star-lab/

For more information, visit BJ-Super7.com

Printed in the USA
CPSIA information can be obtained
at www.ICGtesting.com
JSHW031907180724
66673JS00018B/532

9 781837 963027